A Step-by-Step Guide to
Intimacy with God

DRAWING

CLOSER

GLEN MARTIN &
DIAN GINTER

BROADMAN
& HOLMAN
PUBLISHERS

Nashville, Tennessee

Published by:
Broadman & Holman Publishers
Nashville, Tennessee

Design:
Steven Boyd

4261-82
0-8054-6182-5

Dewey Decimal Classification: 231.7
Subject Heading: Spiritual Life
Library of Congress Card Catalog Number: 94-24526

Unless otherwise noted, Scripture quotations are from the Holy Bible,
New International Version, copyright © 1973, 1978, 1984 by
International Bible Society. Verses marked AMP are from The
Amplified Bible, Old Testament copyright © 1962, 1964 by
Zondervan Publishing House, used by permission, and the New
Testament © The Lockman Foundation 1954, 1958, 1987, used by
permission; KJV, the King James Version; NASB, the New American
Standard Bible, © the Lockman Foundation, 1960, 1962, 1963,
1968, 1971, 1972, 1973, 1975, 1977, used by permission; TLB, The
Living Bible, copyright © Tyndale House Publishers, Wheaton, Ill.,
1971, used by permission.

Library of Congress Cataloging-in-Publication Data
Martin, Glen S., 1953–
    Drawing closer : a step-by-step guide to intimacy with God /
by Glen S. Martin and Dian Ginter.
    p. cm.
    ISBN 0-8054-6182-5
    1. Spiritual life—Christianity. 2. Intimacy (Psychology)—
Religious aspects—Christianity. I. Ginter, Dian, 1939– . II. Title
BV4501.2.M3433 1995
248.4'861—dc20
94-24526
CIP

To the people of Community Baptist Church, who have shared in the work of the ministry and cared so deeply about their own personal drawing closer to God. We thank you for keeping your sacred appointment in attending church each week, ready to listen, ready to grow, ready to serve, and ready to meet with God.

This book is your story and we share it with others with deep appreciation and a heart full of thankfulness.

Contents

◆

Foreword

Something remarkable is happening across our country. This past year has seen thousands of men gathering in stadiums to worship God and to exalt His Son, Jesus Christ. Men and women are attending evangelistic crusades in ever-increasing numbers. Teens by the thousands have attended conferences and are making commitments to live by God's standards of purity and holiness. I've yet to be in a city that doesn't have a group of people gathering for prayer across racial and denominational lines. I believe that what all these people are seeking to see accomplished in their personal lives is exactly what this book is all about, drawing closer to God and subsequently drawing closer to their families and others.

We are seeing something miraculous and supernatural taking place in our nation. We are seeing people renew their zeal and passion for God. Like a mighty wind the Holy Spirit is beginning the process of personal renewal and revitalization in hundreds of lives. And in the midst of God's handiwork, we are seeing many receiving Christ as their personal Savior. We are also seeing thousands who no longer are satisfied with the dynamics of their relationship with the Lord, desiring to deepen their walk and sensing a closeness to God unlike they have ever experienced.

If you have found yourself in one of these positions or desire a closer walk with the Lord, this book can provide the step-by-step guidance that can change your life. Glen Martin and Dian Ginter have put together a book which is not only an intellectual exercise when read; it is also a practical "hands-on" guide designed to move a reader through the maze of uncertainty in knowing about God's sovereignty to an ever-deepening sense of secure friendship based upon understanding God's attributes, and how His character will allow you to trust Him in every area of your life.

As you read, be prepared to make those sacrifices necessary for you to become the man or woman God wants you to be. Be prepared to take small steps at first, while making giant leaps for eternity, for you will never be the same. You are about to embark on a journey unlike any you have traveled, and you will see that drawing closer is the road to genuine joy and ultimate security.

E. Glenn Wagner, Ph.D.
Vice-president, National Ministries
Promise Keepers

How to Use
This Book

*F*or those wanting to get the most out of *Drawing Closer: A Step-by-Step Guide to Intimacy with God,* we suggest you begin reading through for understanding and an overview of where you are going. Get the big picture. You may find it helpful to have pen and paper next to you (or your computer if you are really into the twenty-first century!) so you can record your thoughts and observations. Start doing the steps suggested at the level you identify as your relationship with God. But also continue to the end of the book.

Next, go back to those parts that you have yet to complete on your walk. Have you completed to your own satisfaction all steps in the previous levels? If not, decide if you should continue at the level you have identified, or if you need to strengthen these weak places in the earlier levels first. This decision will in part depend on your nature and how you function. Do you mind having some things not completed before starting a new area, or are you able to start something new while working on a previous, minor area at the same time?

What you get from this book will be entirely up to you. How much you are willing to follow what is shown without making excuses or saying, "I am an exception to this because . . . " will determine the degree to which this material will impact your life.

You must realize that the enemy does not want you to do any of this. He will put up a good fight to make you undervalue, criticize, and otherwise ignore this material. So, even before you start, we suggest you pray similar to the following:

> *Dear God,*
> *I want to know You more, to really draw closer to You, and to have as meaningful a relationship as possible. I've tried, but I have never seemed that successful. You know what it will take. Please speak to me through this book and teach me what You want me to learn from it. Then help me to apply it and to enjoy the process. Draw me closer to You. Let my mind and heart be one with Yours. Keep me on track.*

Our prayer is that as you read this book, your understanding will be opened even more to how special you are to the Lord and how much He wants to have you draw closer to Him no matter where you may be in the process right now. We desire that you become so hungry for this relationship that you will do whatever it takes to have it. And finally, we pray that the tools we have supplied you for this venture will help you do just that.

Of course, to cover such a broad, rich area is impossible in one book. Because of the great need in the body for this type of book now, we tried giving you an overview to whet your appetite to go deeper and wider on your own. You may want to give us your insights, personal testimonies, ideas, or anything else the Lord is teaching you in this area, or you may have suggestions of other areas to explore. We welcome your comments. Address all correspondence to Dr. Glen Martin and Miss Dian Ginter, Community Baptist Church, 1243 Artesia Blvd., Manhattan Beach, CA 90266.

You may also contact Dian for special services such as creating specific materials for you and/or your church, designed for your needs in whatever area you request help. Her expertise is in three main areas: prayer, teaching, and counseling. She has developed a number of simple yet powerful counseling aides. Her fax is 909-864-0132 or telephone 909-862-3467.

May God bless you as you learn to draw closer to Him. We are praying for you.

♦

The Waiting Friend

*T*he individual waited patiently, hoping the beloved friend would be there soon. What a great friendship they had. How much they enjoyed their times of talking and sharing experiences, of sorting out problems and their solutions—of just sharing life together. Their times with each other were the highlight of the day for both. Yet lately something seemed to be changing. The waiting figure knew the problem, but waited anyway. As the minutes slipped by—first one hour and then two—with still no sign, the figure bowed in sorrow, realizing that again the time for meeting that morning had passed.

Well, maybe during the friend's lunch break there might be a quick chance to chat, to share what had been going on since their last talk. Yet again only silence. No contact. Then joy lit up the person's face when the friend came into the room. But it was only a brief visit to ask for some help on a project. Gladly, the help was given. They exchanged quick niceties, agreeing to meet that evening when things would be less hectic and they could spend some quality time together as they loved doing.

Again, disappointment. He heard only a mumbled, "Late night at work. Hope it's okay. I'm dead tired. Let's talk in the morning when I'm fresh. Night." The next morning saw a repeat of the day before. Things kept crowding out any time for the friends to meet, to talk, to fellowship. Oh, there were always good intentions, but always in a rush, with rarely anything meaningful. The waiting friend's heart was heavy, for the longing to see the beloved friend was deep and intense. But patience was strong, so each day saw a repeat or variation of these scenes.

Once in a great while the friends really connected, and it was a delightful, refreshing time for both. The neglectful friend would go away rejoicing in the time, vowing to be regular in his contacts. But the pattern of neglect kept repeating with days turning into weeks, weeks into months. And so it went until even the casual contacts were fewer and far between. The loving friend waited alone, longing for fellowship with the one who had been so close to Him. His eyes looked out over all the friends that surrounded Him, but He rarely saw the object of His search. Yes, many friends, but He missed this one in a *special* way.

God waits. We grow cold. Problems arise. Why does a once bright fire of warm friendship burn down, cool off? Is it done on purpose? Rarely. There is usually some small, yet significant reason why. Just as sand in the works of a fine tuned instrument can damage, even destroy the smooth workings of the motor, so little things can creep into our relationship with God. We hardly even notice them at first. Though as fine as the fine sands on the beach, these things are real and can create havoc in our relationship with God. A simple problem, a grain of disappointment, an unchecked thought that lets in a crack of doubt, a speck of laziness, a drop of carelessness—all these and much more can create the atmosphere for us to lose our first love.

♦

PART ONE

Drawing Closer

Chapter 1

The Necessity
of Drawing Closer

*H*ave you ever seen a Christian friend who had such a wonderful relationship with the Lord that you were almost envious? Did you think to yourself, *Oh, how I wish I knew God in that way and could hear from God as my friend does. But I know I never will. I can never be as deserving as this person, or good enough for God to let me be that close to Him. . . ?* Such puzzling thoughts are not uncommon among believers. But are the conclusions right?

God created us with the need for relationship. We need God and each other. We need to feel appreciated, important, and significant to God and to others. When these things are missing, depression, despair, and even suicide are not far away. For many, though, this concept is like a giant, complicated God-puzzle in which they have a lot of puzzle pieces, but no accurate picture from which to work to put the puzzle properly together. Throughout the centuries, people have tried putting their pieces together, often coming up with distorted, unsatisfying pictures which never fill the need they sense is missing in their own life—a missing puzzle piece which in essence is God.

Those who start to put the pieces together correctly soon notice it takes the shape of a road, the road of life. Makes sense, doesn't it, for God is with us on the road, desiring to go with us, show us the best ways, point out the obstacles. The picture is one that, when completed, will be our life with God. He is involved in every part, every aspect. Each day has its puzzle piece to put in, and each day should give us a better, fuller understanding of who God is as we see Him working in our lives, as we learn more about Him from His Word, the Bible, and start experiencing closer, deeper levels of relationship with Him.

In World War II the Chinese controlled their prisoners by causing them to isolate themselves. How? One key factor was to have prisoners tell about their past, beginning with innocent, good memories, and then moving to a "true confession" time. Added to that was encouragement to inform on each other.

In so doing, for most there came a point at which each prisoner suddenly had the feeling he had said too much. Withdrawal symptoms set in, and they avoided opening up to each other, afraid of what might be said or done in retaliation to humiliate them. Huddled, lone figures eventually could be seen in the prison compounds, men who had chosen to wall themselves off from each other, not trusting anyone, withdrawn and a threat to no one. Few guards were needed once this state had been reached.

Such a plan can truly be said to be diabolical. The master evil one in the universe has long used such plans successfully with mankind, both the saved and the unsaved. But for our purposes, let's look at how he manipulates the unsuspecting individual who falls into the enemy trap by isolating himself from God or from any meaningful, deeper level of intimacy with the Creator. Too often the enemy of our souls gives us wrong puzzle pieces to distort whatever picture we are forming about God and His thoughts and intentions towards us.

Satan tries to get us suspicious of God, to fear Him, to question His goodness and care for us, to mistrust Him in His desire to help us. Some people, who are truly born again but are not in a close relationship with God, are afraid to commit themselves to God and His plans for their lives. They believe He may impose on them some terrible thing they will definitely not want to do and be miserable in doing if they follow His leading.

Those who truly know their God recognize such thoughts as a lie from the pit of hell. Those with a close, loving, warm, meaningful relationship with God have found Him to be the most wonderful, caring, desirable Person to know and very worthy of trusting their life and future in His hands. Some "privileged" people have such a close relationship with the Lord that they almost radiate His presence in their countenances. They definitely seem to have solved the God-puzzle.

Coauthor, Dian, has a dear friend, David, who is just such a person. "Growing up I remember always being happy when David would visit us. He was great to be around. His personality was so sweet and kind, yet he was a very sharp, deep thinker. My father used to say, 'To hear David pray is as though you were listening in on a conversation between best friends. David knows his God!' Looking back I can see that indeed David does know the Lord in an intimate, personal way that has no barriers to it, pouring out his thoughts to his Friend, yet in a very reverential and proper manner. I recall longing to know God in such a way as I listened to his unpretentious, warm prayers. David set the standard for my prayer life. But it would be years before I reached it, not for lack of desire, but simply because I didn't know how to. I had all the puzzle pieces, but my understanding of how to put the puzzle pieces together was weak."

For many this is true. Too often we think, *Oh, I could never be that way in prayer. Such people are special, favored people. I'm just ordinary. God would never want such an intimate relationship with me. I really am nobody.* And we don't pursue the quest because we buy into the lies of the enemy—lies that are as old as the Garden of Eden. Eve heard similar words about God when Satan tempted her. She undoubtedly was made to feel God really didn't care about her as much as He said He did. We can almost hear her thinking, in agreement with the tempter, *Isn't God withholding this wonderful fruit which would make us like Him? Isn't He really just being selfish and even jealous that we will become like Him if we eat of the fruit? What an unloving, two-faced thing to do! We have a right to eat of this! I'm in control of my life. I'll do as I please!*

And so sin entered the world as our first parents bought the lie of God being less than the good, trustworthy, wonderful, loving, caring Individual He truly is. They accepted, without questioning, a flawed puzzle piece from the enemy of their souls. And that piece has distorted for millions throughout the intervening years the true image of a loving, kind, caring Friend. In its place has come the distorted picture of a coldhearted, uncaring, cruel, often capricious god who is just waiting to pounce on us if we violate his rules. False puzzle pieces have been substituted—the lies for the true ones. We have identified some of these substitute pieces:

GOD IS / HAS	SATAN'S LIES ABOUT GOD
Unconditional love	Conditional love, unloving
Accepting	Rejecting, suspicious of us
Source of security	Someone to fear
Trustworthy	Unreliable, capricious
Giving	Withholds desirable things, stingy
Selfless	Self-centered, manipulator
Caring	Indifferent toward man, distant
Just	Unfair, partial
Good	Evil

Satan always tries to attack our relationship with God in order to keep us from getting to know who He is and what He really is like. Our enemy knows that once we really understand what a great, mighty, personal, loving, kind God He is, we will fall so deeply in love with Him and trust Him so completely, that our lives will be transformed and in the process become a real threat to all of Satan's plans. Prayer will be enhanced, clean living will result, and good works will flow out from such individuals—including effectively sharing with the lost about the love and forgiveness of their wonderful Friend.

Catch the Vision: The Purpose of This Book

Many people realize that having an intimate friendship with God is possible, yet they have little idea how to begin. In fact, they don't know what level their relationship is presently on nor do they know how to improve it. The purpose of this book is to help you understand the different levels of knowing God, to identify where you are in this process, and finally to give you effective suggestions on how to go from where you are to where you want to be—in essence, how to solve the God-puzzle.

One of the key elements in this journey will be prayer. We like Richard Foster's definition: "Prayer is nothing more than an ongoing and growing love relationship with God the Father, Son, and Holy Spirit."[1]

Relationships are a choice. God has chosen and offered to each of His children the ability to be as close to Him as David, who had an intimate understanding and friendship with God (1 Sam. 13:14); as close as Enoch, who walked with God in such fellowship that God one day "took" him home so he never experienced death (Gen. 5:24, AMP); as near as Abraham who was called a friend of God (James 2:23); or any other great saint throughout the ages. No matter who you are, how terrible your past, with God's help, you can be changed, and reach such heights in your walk and relationship with God.

Jim Voss is just such a man. He was a mobster in the 1940s, but once the Lord took hold of his life, this man was changed as dramatically as a caterpillar is into a beautiful butterfly. He became someone God could use powerfully in the Billy Graham crusades for many decades. His testimony of how God touched his life has impacted many.

Chuck Colson is another example of a highly successful man, centered in his own world, who had little problem in compromising if to him the end justified the means. However, since meeting Jesus in prison, his life has been transformed. He now lives for God, holds strong moral convictions, and invests his life in those who are behind bars, helping them become spiritually free as he now is. When Chuck speaks on morality, people listen, for his biblically-based ethics are right on target and irrefutable. His strong relationship with the Lord is a key part of who he has become today.

As you read this book we hope that you will have the following experiences:

- Glimpse what you have been missing.
- Catch a vision of the great friendship you could have with God if you take the necessary steps.
- See the great benefit that will come to you from doing so.
- Enjoy the pure pleasure in getting to know such an awesome, personal God.
- Understand how to take these steps and start to do just that.
- No longer feel confused about the God-puzzle, but confident in your picture of God and in your ability to complete accurately your picture of Him.

THE PROGRESSION

God has placed a desire for Himself within the human heart. Romans 1 explains that we know about God's existence not only from external evidences, such as in nature, but also internally with our knowledge that He must exist. Each person chooses how he will respond to such knowledge. Those who choose to pursue Him, find Him and the rewards are great. We start out by:

- Knowing He exists
- Experiencing salvation
- Having as close a relationship as we are willing to develop.

It all depends on us. God has provided everything that is necessary for the deepest of intimate relationships with Him.

One spring day a tornado touched down in West Texas near Paul's home. He was only three or four years old. At the first hint of trouble his father hustled all the children inside, laid them and their mother on the floor together, and covered them with a mattress. His father explained that they would be safe there.

But as they waited out the tornado, Paul realized his father had not climbed under the mattress with them. Paul peeked out to discover his dad standing at the window, watching the funnel cloud turn and twist across the prairie.

When Paul saw his father by the window, he knew where he wanted to be. He struggled out of his mother's arms, crawled out from under the mattress, and then ran and wrapped his arms around his dad's leg.

Recalling that day years later Paul said, "Something told me that the safest place to stand in a storm was next to my father."[2] It sounds like there's a sermon there, doesn't it? Perhaps something about trusting our Heavenly Father. Something about recognizing that He is continually there waiting for us to spend time with Him.

It has always been God's desire to have a close relationship with humans. This is what He had with Adam and Eve in Genesis 3:8 when He walked in the Garden with them. Both God and the first couple enjoyed deep fellowship, but sin put a damper on that and has ever since. Still some people seemed to have found such a sweet relationship.

Genesis 5:24 tells us that Enoch walked with God. There was such fellowship between them that one day he walked straight into heaven! Abraham was a "friend" of God (Isa. 41:8).

He wasn't perfect, but his life was pleasing to God, and his commitment and trust in the Lord were strong. Moses had the privilege of talking to God "face to face, as a man speaks with his friend" (Ex. 33:11).

Many of the psalms written by David reveal he was a man who loved God deeply. We see his heart in Psalm 63:1–6:

> O God, you are my God, earnestly I seek you; my soul thirsts for you, my body longs for you, in a dry and weary land where there is no water . . .
>
> Because your love is better than life, my lips will glorify you. I will praise you as long as I live, and in your name I will lift up my hands. My soul will be satisfied as with the richest of foods; with singing lips my mouth will praise you. On my bed I remember you; I think of you through the watches of the night.

David was enraptured with God. His trust in Him, illustrated in the killing of Goliath, and his longing after God as seen throughout the Psalms all indicate a rich relationship with the Lord. Yet he, too, had his ups and downs. Still his heart was set toward God, and he desired to please Him in all he did, even though he was not perfect. God honored him for his heart's attitude and resulting relationship by calling David a man after God's own heart (1 Sam. 13:14).

HEART ATTITUDE IS THE KEY

Our heart attitude plays a pivotal role in determining how close we will draw to God and at what rate. This is why God wants us to get to know Him better. The better we know Him, the more we will trust Him as we see His great capabilities and experience His power working in and through our lives. Closeness comes as we yield ourselves to Him in trust.

But how does one go about drawing closer to God? Does it just happen over a period of time? Are there steps that can be taken to enhance our ability to draw closer? What insights can we have?

Well, first of all, intimacy with God is an ongoing process, a very necessary process. We will be examining each step in chapters 3 through 8. The key will be learning more about who God really is, what He can and will do for those He loves, what He thinks about you, and how His heart responds to you.

GOD INITIATES; WE RESPOND

In Jeremiah 29:11–14 the Lord expresses these wonderful words. "For I know the thoughts that I think toward you, saith the LORD, thoughts of peace, and not of evil, to give you an expected end. Then shall ye call upon me, and ye shall go and pray unto me, and I will hearken unto you. And ye shall seek me, and find me, when ye shall search for me with all your heart. And I will be found by you, saith the LORD" (KJV). The New International Version of verse 11 says that the Lord has "plans to prosper you and not to harm you."

As you learn these things and they sink deeply into your heart and soul, your faith and trust in Him will grow. You will want to spend time with Him, not because you ought to, but out of a heart that is awakening to the desire to spend time in talking with God; a heart that is beginning to long for time with its Creator as the Spirit draws you to Him; a heart that is seeking Him with all that is within it.

Lloyd Ogilvie captures the power of this concept in his comment on this Jeremiah passage:

Talk about a conversation opener! Imagine someone you love and admire and whose thoughts and opinions you cherish, saying to you, "You are constantly on my mind. And when I think of you they are wonderful thoughts of peace and future happiness for you. I'm pulling for the very best for you. What a joy it is to be your cheerleader!" It would not be difficult to find time for conversation with a person like that. Multiply the best of human care and concern for us a billion times and you've only begun to fathom God's love for us as He calls us into conversation. That's the whole point of time alone with God. It is to allow Him the opportunity to love us.[3]

As part of His love we would add that God wants also to use this time to lovingly correct and guide us. Dr. Ogilvie then observes something that is so often true: "The desire to pray is the result of His greater desire to have a deep communication of love with us. He's been at work in us. We don't need to get His attention—He wants our attention! Prayer starts with God."[4]

Coauthor, Glen, recalls sharing in a Sunday morning message the story of a man in Lucerne, Switzerland, who went to the summit of Mount Pilatus in a cable car operated by hydraulic power. As he ascended, he marveled at the miracles of modern engineering. More than halfway up, his attention was caught by a waterfall. The water powered down the mountainside. If the railway symbolized modern science, then that waterfall was the symbol of primitive nature. *What a contrast!* he thought. Then it suddenly occurred to him that the waterfall was not a contrast but a complement. It was the source of the hydraulic power. It was the force of that water that was driving him up. So it is with prayer. The power that takes us to God is the same power that comes from God, a beautiful divine circle of prayer. In fact, the illustration below shows how this process works.

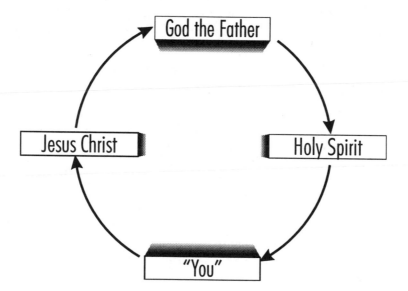

True prayer starts in the heart of God. He then, through the Holy Spirit, communicates this to our heart. We feel a need to pray for what he has communicated—often even thinking that what we are praying for originated in our own heart and mind. Then we pray this back to the Father through the name of the Lord Jesus and the right He gives us to access the Father in prayer, thus completing the circle of prayer. As the Father hears our prayer, He then answers it, since we are praying according to His will.

One of the wonderful by-products of this deepening understanding of God is our prayer life will be richer and more meaningful. We will start praying according to God's will and thus see the promise of 1 John 5:14–15 fulfilled, which in essence says if we ask anything that is according to God's will He not only hears us but answers our prayers.

Answered prayer is a wonder in itself. First, the thing I asked for is done. But as important, it brings such joy and satisfaction as I gain a deepening knowledge that God is there; He is listening and thus acting on my behalf! It increases my faith and trust in Him and my courage to ask for even more that is within His will next time.

Once, when the authors were working on this very book, it looked as if the computer had crashed at just the wrong time. They did everything they could to get the computer back "up" again, but to no avail. Then Dian said, "Lord, You know what's wrong. Please make it work" and it immediately started working perfectly—much to their amazement and joy.

There was nothing fancy about the prayer, and Glen's teasing response of "Why does God always answer your prayers?" was humorous, yet Dian's response was probably closer to the truth. "God answered because He was trying to show me I should have prayed when this first happened, rather than waiting until now when we've done all we could." She knew better and should have asked her Friend's help right away. But she only took that step when she felt at a loss to do anything else. How human! We all do this, don't we?

MISCONCEPTIONS AND WRONG MOTIVES

Because God is not visible, we can forget the wonderful Friend who is there, just waiting to talk with us, to help us, and to give us counsel in each and every aspect of our lives. But we too often are preoccupied, too busy, or just negligent in going to Him. In fact, some people feel they don't want to bother the Almighty God with a little thing like lost keys, small financial problems, relationships, the need for a parking place, etc.

Here we see the first misconception: People want to use their prayers to bring only big problems to God. For some the philosophy is either, "God is too busy running the universe to worry about this small problem I'm having" or "If I ask Him for this, He may not be willing to help me when I really need it. So I'll solve this one myself and run to Him when it is something more important." To such people, it is as though they only have a certain number of "chips" with God; and they must be wise in the way they spend them, lest they run out and not have any when they really need Him. In a similar vein, are people who feel God will be fed up with answering their prayers if they constantly ask Him for things. They don't want to be caught like the little boy who cried "wolf" all the time when there really was no problem, only to find no help when there was a wolf, a big problem.

For others, life has convinced them they are not worth very much, so they conclude God will not be interested in helping them. They feel insignificant and unworthy, so they wonder, why pray? To others, past sin makes them feel unworthy of God's help. Then there are those who have been discouraged in the past when God has said no and have given up on asking God, lest they be disappointed again. Such disappointment would reinforce their already strong feelings of rejection, alienation, and poor self-image. These are just some of the many misconceptions many have about God and their relationship with Him.

Trust and commitment are so difficult when one has any of these misconceptions about God. Satan is the source and wants us to remain unenlightened about how wonderful and satisfying a deep, trusting relationship with God is. If Satan can keep us weak in our faith level, then he can greatly neutralize our effectiveness for the Lord as we maintain a shallow walk with Him.

Many people have very self-centered motives for prayer, for spending time with God. They use Him as a "store" where they bring their shopping list and expect it to be filled. Often this is because they feel they have earned God's favor through doing good things for Him and His people. Therefore, He "owes" answered prayer to them.

Others feel they are so needy that God is obligated to help them even though they may be doing little in the relationship. It is basically a one-way street, with God being the One to give and they to receive. They spend little if any time in worship or in talking to their loving Friend, nor do they feel they need to. "He will understand," they say. "Anyway, He's probably too busy or not interested in what I have to say. Not only that, He already knows all about me, so why bother to tell Him what He already knows." Their motives and misconceptions of how to have a healthy walk with God—if in fact they ever think of such a thing—are badly flawed.

And so relationship is never strengthened, and many a person sadly goes through life with a distorted picture of God, because they have never taken the time to seek Him, to develop a desire for Him, to get to know this awesome God who has reached out to them in love and in turn has been ignored or misunderstood. Like Eve, they have been willing to buy whatever lie about God and themselves is given and have ignored the true picture of God revealed in the pages of Scripture, painted in all of nature, and written in their own hearts.

In a little different context, yet still applicable, Paul wrote in Romans 1:25 about those who have "exchanged the truth of God for a lie, and worshiped and served the created things rather than the Creator." Sometimes we become our own God or we allow the circumstances or people around us to so capture our attention that we have little time for God and thus neglect Him as we focus on His creation. This will happen when our spouse, children, jobs, car, home—even serving in the church—are placed before God in our affections and our priorities.

Now don't get us wrong. We're not saying we shouldn't ask God for things. But the question is our motives. As we explore our deepening relationship with God in chapters 3 through 8, we will see that even though we probably start out with self-centered motives for developing relationship, as we begin to appreciate Him more, get to really draw closer to Him, we will find our basic desire to be seeking His will, seeing His goals accomplished, and only then asking Him for our own needs. Even these will be asked for in the light of His will, desiring only what He wants for us, not what we may perceive to be needed.

How this change in perspective enhances our relationship with Him! It is like a self-centered child always asking his parent for something and never expressing any love or appreciation nor doing anything nice in return. Contrast this to the appreciative, kind, and loving child who seeks to please his parents. He may ask, but not demand. And when he receives, his appreciation is genuine and brings joy to his parent's heart. So it is with our loving Father. He wants to bless us, to fellowship with us; He wants us to know Him in a deeper way. As this happens, our perspective changes from ego-centric to God-centric. When this occurs we are well on our way to an intimate, deepening friendship with Him.

As in so many other ways, Jesus is a wonderful example to us in this area. He had such a close relationship with the Father—not just because He was very God, Himself, but because as 100 percent man He knew He had to spend time with the Father, talking with Him, seeking His face, His will, His blessings.

Jesus confirms this when He said in John 5:30, "By myself I can do nothing; I judge only as I hear." With as busy a life as Jesus had, with as many things as He did in ministry, these words indicate a tremendous amount of time spent listening to the

Father. Often these times were before the sun was up or after a day's ministry. His disciples so sensed the importance of prayer in His life that, even though they were good Jews and knew how to pray, they asked Him to teach them how to pray as He prayed. They must have perceived the close relationship Jesus had with the Father and in turn attributed it, at least in part, to the times He spent in prayer. The depth of His fellowship with the Father was not lost on them.

So, having set the example, Jesus then demonstrated the key to His human relationships. Two words usually overlooked in Mark 3:14 reveal the key. When Jesus appointed the twelve apostles, we read they were to be "with Him." Wow! To be with Jesus twenty-four hours a day! Wouldn't that be wonderful? To watch Him minister, to hear His teachings, to walk with Him, to see Him in unguarded moments, to be discipled and trained by Him. Who wouldn't want that? And yet we have something even better—the Father, the Spirit, *and* Jesus living on the inside of us—in constant communication with us if we will only listen. Yet for many, our relationship with our loving God is sadly like that of the married couple, occupying the same home but having little, if any, real communication. They are like ships that pass in the night. They know each other exists, but that is the extent of their interaction.

So what do we do? That is what this book is all about. We will help you see where you are right now in your walk with the Lord and evaluate how deeply your relationship with Him has developed. Then we will show you how to go from where you are to where you desire to be—the intimate friendship level. We will give you keys to many puzzle pieces and show you how to put them together in a productive way. But remember, just as a tree goes through stages of root development before it may bear the fruit God intended for it, so we must go through a process. Our root system must be drawn to the fountain of living waters and we must sense the fulfillment and excitement God intended for us in our walk of faith. We have developed the tree illustration which follows to help you visualize this process.

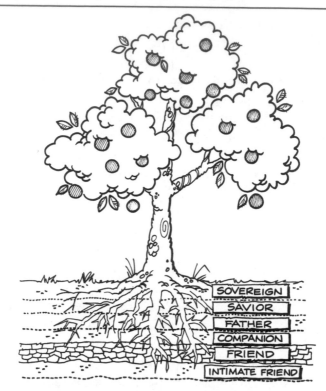

As we go through each level, we will look at some of the specific aspects of God's nature, often called attributes, that people will focus on at that level. We will examine the motivation for obeying Him at the different levels, what the heart response is to Him, how close people will feel toward God, and how this degree of knowing God will affect their interaction with people and probable outlook on life.

Let's take a brief overview of these different levels and the elements involved in each. Realize these are simply guidelines. We recognize there will be a blending between the levels as people respond in their own particular way because of their own backgrounds, personalities, giftings, and experiences.

◆

Level 1: *Holy Sovereign*

A. Attributes and qualities of God most observed by the person: Creator, majesty, all powerful, present everywhere, wise, all knowing, holy, King, eternal, infinite

B. Obedience based on fear, but still wants to control his own destiny.

C. Closeness to God: *Arm's Length* (Would not embrace Him).

D. Heart's response to God: curiosity, worship, awe, recognition of His authority. May be afraid not to obey God, still seeing God as impersonal. Seeking truth but not yet surrendered (Holy Spirit is drawing the person).

E. Main focus of prayer: *Self-centered* (What I can get out of the relationship.)

F. Effect of relationship with God on actions with others: *Limited.*

G. Outlook on life: Self-centered, insecure. Probably hopeless.

Level 2: *Forgiving Savior*

A. Additional attributes and qualities of God most observed: Good, loving, caring, merciful, sacrificial, forgiving, accepting, intermediator, gentle.

B. Obedience based on: Thankfulness, gratitude. There will be the start of love and trust.

C. Closeness to God: Heart kneeling in surrender

D. Heart's response to God: Thankful, love, overwhelmed, desire to obey. Learning to praise and worship. Sense areas needing change and surrender. Will start to read the Word and pray, but may or may not get a strong hunger to do either. Trust starting to grow. Will depend on background, personality, and how trusting by nature.

E. Main focus of prayer: Pray because one "ought to," but also out of love.

F. Effect of relationship with God on actions with others: Starting to change, to be more Spirit-controlled but still probably self-centered in motivation.

G. Outlook on life: Excitement about new life. Feeling clean. Anticipation

Level 3: *Loving Father*

A. Additional attributes and qualities of God most observed: Protector ♦ Provider ♦ Patient ♦ Discipler ♦ Accepting Teacher ♦ Helper ♦ Nurturing ♦ Accessible ♦ Kind

B. Obedience based on: Necessity

C. Closeness to God: Can "touch" Him; may "sit on His lap," with His arm around you.

D. Heart's response to God: Realize God is on my side. Some hunger for the Word and to obey it. Increasing desire to obey God, yet areas still not yielded. Trust is growing, but . still not full. Feeling of belonging to God as a child.

E. Main focus of prayer: Prayer based on right thing for spiritual health, get own needs met, and for those they are about.

F. Effect of relationship with God on actions with others: May be less nervous and have more self-control in difficult situations and when disagreements come, because growing self-confidence through relationship with God is making the person feel less threatened.

G. Outlook on life: More secure and optimistic, faith growing.

Level 4: *Faithful Companion*

A. Additional attributes and qualities of God most observed: Fair/just, compassionate, wonderful, encourager, peace giver, counselor, faithful, empowerer giving, trustworthy

B. Obedience based on: Love

C. Closeness to God: Hand in hand

D. Heart's response to God: Deepening love and trust in God. Wants to please God. Becoming more submissive to God's will; struggling less. Greater ability to praise. Word becoming more understandable. Growing sense of the presence of God and His love and acceptance. Intensifying desire to draw closer to Him, to trust Him more, and to please Him. Will surrender most areas, yet will still have some reservations about total commitment.

E. Main focus of prayer: Worship and praise will intensify. Starting to seek God's agenda in prayer more than before.

F. Effect of relationship with God on actions with others: More consistent fruit of the Spirit being manifested on a regular basis, especially self-control, peace, and joy.

G. Outlook on life: Sense of feeling secure and confident.

During these first three to four levels, there will most likely be self-centered motivation for the relationship—how it makes me feel, what I can get out of it, a wonderful way to get my needs met, I feel so good when I am accepted and loved. But as we move into the fourth and definitely by the fifth levels, we will begin experiencing a shift of focus as we become less self-centered and more God-centered.

Richard Foster explains it this way: "In the beginning we are indeed the subject and the center of our prayers. But in God's time and in God's way a Copernican revolution takes place in our heart. Slowly, almost imperceptibly, there is a shift in our center of gravity. We pass from thinking of God as part of our life to the realization that we are part of His life. Wondrously and mysteriously God moves from the periphery of our prayer experience to the center. A conversion of the heart takes place, a transformation of the spirit."[5]

As this shift comes, no longer will we go to Him just to receive or to "feel good." Now we will be with Him because He is so wonderful, so desirable. As part of this transition we will desire to spend time with Him, not because it is the best thing for us, like taking vitamins or eating our spinach and Brussels sprouts—but rather we will have a yearning to go to Him, a drawing deep within us that compels us to draw closer, to spend time. Our hearts will want to please Him and the way we live will be affected not only in our relationship with Him, but with others.

You will notice the tree diagram on page 20 depicts a stone wall which reflects resistance to roots going deeper. Such obstacles can be ego, mistrust of God, misconceptions, fears, or a desire to still maintain some control of life. The enemy will come in with lies such as, "If you totally surrender, you will just be a doormat." or "You have certain rights and expectations. Don't let them get taken away" to encourage the individual not to trust God fully and to maintain some degree of control. That is why we call faith and trust the taproot of our spiritual life. Our spiritual life will only be as healthy as the faith-trust taproot is strong.

This level is often one at which many Christians unfortunately stop because they are unwilling to make the necessary sacrifice to go on. They sadly miss out on all God has for them in a richer, more satisfying walk with Him.

People have to determine in their hearts they will go deeper, push through their natural, human resistance for absolute trust and submission, and set aside their barrier of ego so they may go deeper into fully knowing and experiencing the intimate depths of our Lord.

Level 5: *Good Friend*

A. Additional attributes and qualities of God: Great wisdom, perfection, tough love-giver, purity, great faithfulness, gracious, unselfish, unchanging, dependable, comforter.

B. Obedience based on: Deep love for God and desire to do His will

C. Closeness to God: Arm in arm

D. Heart's response to God: Desire to obey completely, yet may do so with some feeling of obligation rather than an overwhelming ability to trust the Lord and desire to please Him. As God asks of us a closer walk and stripping away of unsuitable areas of the life, there will be obedience, but often can be a struggle before submitting completely.

The Scriptures are more alive and "sweeter" to the individual. Deepening praise and worship result. Wanting what pleases God is more important than this person's own desires. Roots have gone very deep into the Lord. Faith in Him is becoming very strong, to the point others cannot easily pull the person away from what God wants them to do or think. Only a few things may still be withheld from unconditional surrender.

E. Main focus of prayer: Views quality time with the Lord as very important. Sensitive to the voice of God. Prayer more and more God centered because the individual's desires are being conformed to what God wants.

F. Effect of relationship with God on actions with others: May find people seeking their advice because of their walk with the Lord and resulting wisdom. Desire to walk sin free. Will go the extra mile to maintain a Christ-honoring relationship with others who may be difficult.

G. Outlook on life: Deepening peacefulness in life no matter what the circumstances. Although people may recognize their weaknesses and have not yet corrected them, there is a desire to do so and they are seeking the Lord's help in overcoming their shortcomings.

Note: The difference between "good Friend" and "intimate Friend" for the individual is a fine line. It basically is the degree of trust, faith, commitment, and surrender. It is a line some people cross quickly, while others take more time.

The "good Friend" relationship is one which always reserves the right to say no. The "intimate Friend" has come to the point of absolute surrender because they are so convinced of the goodness and sovereignty of God, that they trust Him no matter what their human feelings may be.

Level 6: *Intimate Friend*

A. Additional attributes and qualities of God: Tenderhearted, gentleness, great heart of love, complete ability to meet every need and care, absolute sovereign and in total control, awesome, absolutely, trustworthy, totally good, wants the very best for me, is completely committed to me.

B. Obedience based on: Deep heart desire to please the Lord in every area of life.

My heart's desire

C. Closeness to God: Inseparable—never leave each other's presence. Always communicating. Feelings much the same as to a spouse.

D. Heart's response to God: Praise, worship, and expressions of love are constantly being expressed. They are used often as a response in times of difficulty to strengthen faith and trust. Overwhelming awe, joy, and excitement at their relationship and how sweet it is. It brings great satisfactions. Thoughts of it can bring tears of joy and gratitude. Life lived to please the Lord. His desires placed above own. Joyous and absolute surrender to every wish of God. No struggle in submission; done immediately. Absolute faith and trust. Strong sense of His presence and friendship at all times. Nothing withheld from the Lord for Him to deal with. Sin is dealt with immediately and grieves the person greatly, for there is a strong desire to do nothing wrong, to live a squeaky clean life. Little things once overlooked or compromised are no longer tolerated. May be some significant fine tuning of the life by God in order to strip away small things that are hindrances in the person's growth and relationship with Him. Such things may seem insignificant to other believers who have not drawn this close, but are seen by these people as something they gladly give up for the One they love so much.

E. Main focus of prayer and relationship with God: Prayer life is a constant flow throughout the day as though the Lord were visible. Prayers less for self and more for what is on the heart of God. Rarely will pray anything outside God's will since the person so senses what God wants and thus prays these concerns back to Him.

F. Effect of relationship with God on actions with others: Great modification of pre-Christian behavior. Control of the Spirit and His fruit flowing through the person is so evident that there is usually a great softness, as well as strength, in the individual. Strong desire to live at peace with everyone. Seen as a person of great wisdom and self control, one who is sought for advice.

G. Outlook on life: Strong faith causes the person to be very optimistic and have a deep trust in God's absolute control of all things. Negative circumstances have less ability to get them off balance. Fear is almost unknown because they look at the Lord and not their circumstances.

Well, have you identified where you think you are? Do you feel a little overwhelmed by all that's left to do? Maybe you are thinking it is almost impossible? That this is only for the "special, holy, perfect people—not someone with all your hang ups? But listen to the wise words of a godly French woman who lived many hundreds of years ago: "This way of prayer, this simple relationship to your Lord, is so suited for everyone; it is just as suited for the dull and the ignorant as it is for the well-educated. This prayer, this experience which begins so simply, has as its end a totally abandoned love to the Lord. Only one thing is required—*Love.*"[6] And she is right. For when we love, there is nothing we won't do for our beloved.

So, don't give up. Believe this is for you. Catch the vision for what God wants in your relationship with Him, and then let us show you step by step how to get from where you are to where you want to be—having an intimate Friend in God. The journey is well worth taking. Each step you take will bring its own satisfaction, and the rewards will be overwhelming and awesome as you draw closer to Him. Throughout we will give you simple, sample prayers, like the following to help you take these steps.

Lord,
I see where I want to be, but, oh, how far I feel from it. I
want to draw closer to You. I desire this more than I can
even put into words. Yet there is so much that screams at
me that I can't be what I've just read. Help me to silence
those lies and to believe that with Your help I can indeed
do all things through You as You strengthen me, as You
promised in Philippians 4:13. As I read the rest of this book,
teach me, Holy Spirit, what I need to understand about my
relationship with the Lord. Teach me how to draw closer to
the One who is my very life and reason for existence.

Amen

Please note. We do not mean to suggest that reaching any of these levels brings perfection or that you can eventually be without problems. Quite the contrary is true. There is always the flesh to contend with, always the weaknesses inherent in our humanity. But such weaknesses do not have to dominate us. We can control them.

Know also that as you draw closer to God, the enemy of your soul will step up his fight to draw you away from God. But remember that he has no ability to win—only to harass you. In Christ we are victorious when we let Him live His life in and through us. That is why 1 John 4:4 is so reassuring: "Greater is he that is in you, than he that is in the world" (KJV).

It is also true that God will shine His light on some of those dark corners of your life that you have hidden. Even though this will bring its own struggles, you will draw closer to Him as you allow Him to remove those hindrances and distractions in your walk.

A Sunday School teacher once asked her students to talk about how they felt about their church. The students responded in the usual ways: Some said something silly to get the rest of the class to laugh, while others tried to be more serious.

One of the girls was new to the class. She felt uncomfortable about entering into class discussions, so she never raised her hand or volunteered an answer. That Sunday, however, she did have an answer for her Sunday School teacher, and it was unforgettable. She said that going to church was "like walking into the heart of God."[7]

What a thought! To be in the very heart of God! Yet this is what He offers us when we approach Him with the proper attitude and desire to know Him better.

We will find the results of drawing closer to God are life-changing. The desirability is obvious. The impact of a changed life for the kingdom of God and against the world's system controlled by Satan is also self-evident. That is why he will do everything in his power to keep you from drawing closer to God. His game plan is unchanged from the Garden of Eden until today.

◆

1. Richard J. Foster, *Prayer: Finding the Heart's True Home* (San Francisco, Calif.: Harper, 1992), 13.

2. Max Lucado, *In the Eye of the Storm* (Dallas: Word Publishing, 1991), 201–202.

3. Lloyd John Ogilvie, *Conversation with God* (Eugene, Ore.: Harvest House Publishers, 1993), 13.

4. Ibid.

5. Foster, op cit., 15.

6. Madame Guyon, *Experiencing the Depths of Jesus Christ* (Goleta: Christian Books, 1975), 47.

7. Dick Van Dyke, *Faith, Hope and Hilarity* (New York: Doubleday and Company, Inc., 1970), 95.

Chapter 2

Elements of Your Spiritual Journey

*T*he words "You're going the wrong way" strike terror in the hearts of most men, because it is not part of their nature to ask for directions. Such was the case when Glen and his family attended a convention in Orlando, Florida, and enjoyed some vacation time together. Since they were staying at a large hotel less than five miles away from Walt Disney World, they had planned on spending one of their free days together seeing this attraction.

Getting there was no problem; getting home was the disaster. After making a wrong turn and getting on the wrong freeway, the family watched as they drove right past their hotel. Of course, the kids were quick to point out Glen's misguided decision. No problem, they decided. All that had to be done was to get off the freeway, turn around, and head back to the hotel.

The difficulty arose when he found there was no exit, so they headed back to Disney World.

Getting off the freeway, turning the car around, getting back on the freeway ready to make the correct decision this time, Glen finally headed back to the hotel. Since this was not happening as quickly as the kids wanted, they kept reminding him it was dinner time. At times like these we wish we could just veer off the main roads and cut across the field to get home, but there are no shortcuts in life. In fact to do so, we'd probably get stuck in a ditch and be in a worse mess than handling a little teasing in the car and its subsequent embarrassment.

Even so, no one could believe it when Glen made the same mistake, heading away from the hotel, a second time. As the family roared at his sense of direction, his wife Nancy uttered those infamous words, "You're going the wrong way." Yet Glen refused to ask for directions. Do you know that Glen made the same error a *third* time? By now everyone in the car was laughing and having a great time making jokes such as, "Maybe we'll never get back," or "We sure have this direction figured out, huh, Dad?"

Many of us are like Glen when it comes to our spiritual journey. We would rather do it ourselves and not ask the help of others. Although most sincere Christians want to know God in a more personal way, in the hurry and bustle of the almost twenty-first century, they sometimes get lost in the journey. Many do not even know where to start. Oh, true, the Bible would be a good starting place, but which one of those sixty-six books? This chapter will help you identify where you are in the process of drawing closer, and then show you how to map out a course for a successful completion of the journey.

To many, drawing closer is a real puzzle. They may have a lot of information—puzzle pieces—but they are not sure what the completed picture looks like. Most do not have the "cover to the box with the picture on it." So even if they have some puzzle pieces, they are uncertain how to use them or even if there are more pieces. Frankly speaking, most people do not have all of them. So they do the best with what they have. They really want to complete the drawing closer picture in their life, but are fuzzy on the details of how to do it.

Chapter 1 outlined the six levels to an intimate relationship with God. This chapter will introduce the roles of faith, fact, and the Holy Spirit in developing this relationship. As you work through eighty-eight questions, you will be able to determine where you are in the six levels of drawing closer to God. Your puzzle will be taking shape. From there you will be given Action Steps for each level that will help you to put the drawing closer puzzle together in an orderly fashion.

But please note, these steps are just suggestions. There is no magic formula to guarantee an automatic intimate relationship with God. But we can show you what has worked for others and make certain suggestions concerning your heart attitude. Remember, if you want to draw close to God—and this is something He wants—then it will happen. He promises that if you draw closer to Him then He will draw closer to you (James 4:8).

ELEMENTS OF EACH LEVEL

Before we begin, we need to examine the common elements in each of the six levels and why they are important.

- *The tree diagram.* Each level except the first has a tree which depicts the Christian's spiritual life, growth, and fruit that come as one progresses in his or her relationship with God. At the first level, relationship is just a seed, for it has not yet been established. There is only the potential of a tree within the seed. But when it is planted into the soil of the Word as the person learns about God as Holy Sovereign, the seed begins to germinate. At the second level relationship starts, represented by a sapling which puts its roots down deeper into the knowledge of who God is and what His desires are as revealed in the rich soil of His Word and the Christian's resulting experience with Him. Each of the next four levels find the tree's roots going deeper, giving strength and growth to the tree which in turn produces more leaves or blessings, and fruit, which is the fruit of the Spirit. The taproot of the tree is the believer's faith and trust in God. This taproot will be very important to the health of the tree, for a weak taproot can damage the growth process.

One of the wonderful things about the Bible is how a new believer can read it and understand what is said—definitely not all the depths of meanings—but ample to be meaningful in one's spiritual infancy.

As you grow in your faith and start to draw closer to the Lord, you should find you never get bored with the Word. Even believers for sixty years will find new facets of understanding as they go deeper into the Word and get more and more spiritual nourishment from it.

The tree diagram illustrates this truth at level. The tree grows and flourishes as the roots go deeper into the soil, picking up new nourishment and more strength at each level. The tree can produce fruit and leaves only as long as it continues to receive fresh nourishment. In the same way, believers find that staying for any length of time at one plateau negatively affects their walk with the Lord.

- *Attributes and qualities of God most observed.* In dealing with humans, God has always revealed Himself in a progressive way, rather than with a full revelation all at one time. Therefore, at each level certain attributes will naturally stand out because of the nature of that level. Each level's attributes will build on the preceding one and will add more pieces to the puzzle of knowing God in a closer, deeper way. At level 1 are the impersonal attributes—power, creator, authority—but each level will find Him becoming more personal.

Tim Stafford has captured the impact getting to know God should have in our lives. He said, "God is different. He is indeed better than we are. The more of His personality we know, the more we will break into astonished praise. Does a 'personal relationship with God' bring God down to our level as a sort of cosmic buddy? Only if the personal relationship is just talk. When the relationship is real, it forces us to our knees. The farther in we go, the higher our eyes will be raised."[1]

We agree. As you go from level to level you indeed will draw closer and have a sweeter, more genuine friendship with God, but you should never lose the wonder or the awe of Who He is and the elements of sovereignty and holiness that are there. It is a delicate balance not to become presumptive, but maintaining such a balance is well worth the effort.

- *Motivation for obedience.* As you go from level to level you will find at first you obey God out of fear, a type of external motivation. But as relationship is established and deepened, you will finally obey Him out of an overwhelming love and desire to please Him, a deep, internal motivation.

- *Closeness to God.* Level by level we trace the closeness of one's relationship with God from a distant one to finally becoming inseparable.

- *Heart's response to God.* As you go through the levels you should notice changes in the way you respond to God. At the first level there may be more curiosity, doubt, confusion, and probably some yearning to know God. However, once relationship is established at the second level, there will be a lessening of the need for everything to agree with human reasoning as your spiritual life starts developing and touching your heart and emotions. Reasoning is not set aside, but in the drawing closer process, another dimension of spiritual understanding develops that was non-existent at level 1. God always wants to develop faith and trust in Him at the heart level. Too often wanting to understand things from a human perspective leads to walking by sight rather than walking by faith. That is why God says His ways are not our ways, but instead are higher than ours (Isa. 55:9).

- *Main focus of prayer.* Part of the drawing process is a shift in the focus for prayer. It will most likely start in a very self-centered way, as the following diagram shows. With maturity and closeness to God, the scope of the prayer focus will enlarge.

Focus of Prayer

Me
Others
Community
God's Heart Desire

- *Effect of relationship with God on actions with others.* We all have seen the husband and wife that look so much like each other, or the individual who has the same hand and facial expressions as their close friend. When you are with someone a lot, you find your actions and mannerisms start to reflect those of the other person. So it is in our relationship with God. The closer we get to the Lord, the more of His nature we reflect as we let Him influence us.

  The Holy Spirit is giving us more and more of the fruits of the Spirit. For example, we may start out with a small amount of self-control. But as we draw closer, we gain more and more, until self-control is exceedingly strong and a way of life. This means our interactions with others will show more of His love, patience, joy and the like. People will not upset or irritate us as much, and we will be able eventually to handle well even the most difficult situations or personalities. In fact, what is happening is we are becoming more and more like Jesus.

- *Outlook on life.* Any parent of a two-year-old can testify to the absolute self-centered quality of the human heart. Even the parent of the newborn or six-month-old knows that the child has no interest in anything except his or her own welfare. Food had better be served on time, diapers changed regularly, and all other felt needs met in a timely fashion if the adults want to live in any semblance of peace.

But look at this same child five years later and we find a "little helper." Ten years beyond that will reveal a lovely young person giving gifts, doing "surprise" jobs for others, and often pitching in when not asked. Depending on the maturity level the child will still be focused on self, but much less than before.

The ensuing years will find the person becoming more flexible and willing to give up "rights." When the person becomes a parent he or she will often be so sacrificial as to neglect one's own good for that of the family.

So it is with our spiritual life. We start out with a very self-centered outlook on life. As we grow in our walk with the Lord, we will find ourselves shifting from self to others and the Lord. The truly mature believers are strongly focused on the Lord and what He wants. Their lives are centered around His will and His purposes for their lives.

FAITH AND TRUST ARE KEY PIECES

Each level will look at two of the most important parts of the puzzle: faith and trust. Without them the spiritual puzzle will fall apart and never be completed; for they play the role of the tab, and the hole, faith,[2] where you put the tab into.

Faith is confidence in God. Trust is the response or action based upon faith. These two attributes interlock to hold the

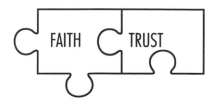

puzzle tightly together. Without them, the puzzle would be composed of only square pieces and thus incapable of holding together.

We are convinced that the strength of faith and trust in God will help move a person through each level. As faith and confidence grow in God—who He is, what He can do, and how He sees you—the drawing closer process is natural. It is like being at the bottom of an equilateral triangle, with God at the top. As a person's faith (confidence in God) on the left side grows and trust (action resulting from faith) on the right side grows, the person gets closer to God.

Notice that faith and trust are on an angle. Anyone who has climbed the side of a mountain knows how an angled slope is slippery without a firm anchor. In the same way, we need to be firmly growing in our relationship with the Lord, who is our Rock, in order to be secure and healthy spiritually. There is no such thing as a static relationship with Him. It is like something floating on the sea; either the object is going toward the shore or away from it.

God has designed a close tie between the Scriptures, faith, and trust. Our faith must originate from the right source or it could be disastrous. Romans 10:17 warns, "Faith cometh by hearing, and hearing by the word of God" (KJV). We must be certain that Scripture is the basic foundation for our faith. Our experience and emotion should agree with what Scripture says. If they do not, those things that contradict the Word must be rejected.

THE PROCESS

Let's look more closely at how this works. From the Scriptures we learn how wonderful and great our God really is. His nature (attributes) and acts are revealed. Faith and trust in Him are strengthened as we learn more about Him and see how He thinks about us. This is also integrated into our talking with Him (prayer) and listening to Him speak to us through the Scriptures, other believers, and inwardly.

Then when we have developed faith in Him because of what the Scriptures say, and are strengthened through our past experiences with Him, we can trust Him in whatever current problems or decisions we are facing. As we see Him work in this situation, keep reading the Word, and observe new facets of His nature, we find a new area in which to trust Him. We step out in faith as our trust allows us to put our faith into action in the current situation. We also see Him honor our trust, so our faith and trust grow together.

It is interesting when you read the Gospels to see how Jesus would teach and/or demonstrate a subject and then give the disciples a chance to put their trust into practice concerning what He just taught. One of our favorite examples of this occurs in Mark. In chapter 6, Jesus had just performed an incredible miracle of feeding the five thousand. Two chapters later He then set up another crisis, giving the disciples an opportunity to trust Him again to feed four thousand.

In chapter 8 He said, "I have compassion for these people; they have already been with me three days and have nothing to eat. If I send them home hungry, they will collapse on the way because some of them have come a long distance" (vv. 2–3). Jesus did not ask them to transform apples into oranges; He asked them to believe that apples could be apples. Yet their reply was: "But where in this remote place can anyone get enough bread to feed them?" (v. 4).

If we were Jesus we might have said, "Hey, guys. Shape up! Didn't you just see Me perform this kind of miracle recently?

Have I suddenly lost My power so that today I can not do what I did then? Where's your faith? Won't you ever learn?" Yes, that is probably how we would have responded. But Jesus, the infinitely patient God/man, instead said, "How many loaves do you have?" (v. 5). He took them back to basics again so their faith could be strengthened.

This is how God is with us. He gives us opportunities to have a deeper faith in Him, to see Him in a new way working in our lives. But if our faith is not developed enough through that circumstance to help us trust Him later on, He simply lets us learn the lesson again through another opportunity.

His usual way of teaching concerns a problem or crisis He allows to come into our lives. The lesson can be learned the first time around rather than creating the need for repeated teaching situations through negative circumstances or people. But too often we want to flee or resist the negative. We want to get away from anything which is uncomfortable or upsetting: the work situation, the nosy neighbor, the difficult marriage. It is much easier to avoid the problem, to flee or ignore the difficult person, than it is to stay and deal with the problem until there is a solution.

Too often we forget that God allowed these negative circumstances into our lives. He is not surprised; He does have a purpose for them to be in our lives. Therefore to resist them or run away from them will cause us to remain in one place, often spinning our spiritual wheels or even going backwards like a wave. We will inevitably be stunted in our growth until we are willing to learn the lesson. Only then can we to grow and draw closer to the Lord.

One thing we need to be aware of in acting on our faith is that the enemy of our souls will do everything he can to undermine our faith and our trust in God. He will

- yell into our ears phrases of doubt

- dredge up our past failures

- plant suspicion and uncertainty

- use the "what if" or "if only" hammers to weaken whatever faith we may have had.

He does not want us to act in trust, but rather pull back in fear or respond in our old doubt-filled ways.

One of the things that happen from level to level is spiritual growth. So let us look at the process a little more closely. The following diagram shows the growth process in a believer's life.

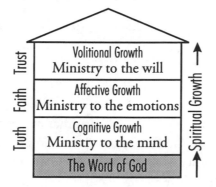

God says that "Faith comes from hearing, and hearing by the word of Christ" (NASB). Already we've seen this close relationship as we learn the truth from God's Word, see faith develop, and finally act based on trust.

We have identified three distinct stages of growth that come from the study of the Word and build upon each other. The first stage is cognitive growth, or an awareness of a truth. We read and understand what is being said. For example, we learned from Romans 8:28 that "All things work together for good to them that love God, to them who are the called according to his purpose" (KJV). We choose to believe this is true, and this produces faith, although as yet untried faith in our lives.

Then comes the time this head knowledge is given the opportunity to produce affective growth as our emotions are brought under the control of our head in the face of a difficult situation. In other words, the situation yells "Panic!" but the Holy Spirit gently but firmly reminds us that He has promised to make even this work together for good.

Thus, our emotions are affected by the Word. We then see our volitional growth occur as we choose not to panic. We choose to put our faith into action by trusting God and not looking at the many negatives that arise when a problem is viewed from a human perspective.

THE IMPORTANCE OF THE HOLY SPIRIT

Before you go to the next chapters, there is one key puzzle piece you need to make sure is in place. Without it, you will never be able to complete the puzzle. It is the equivalent of turning all the pieces right side up. This is the need for believers to have the Holy Spirit in control of their lives moment by moment.

It is only through the Holy Spirit that we are able to live our lives according to God's ways. He alone knows what each day will hold and how we should respond to each part of it. It is as though the Holy Spirit were handing us puzzle pieces to make our day complete.

If at any time we reject the piece He offers and decide to try a different piece that looks as good, we can do it, and sometimes we may even find it fits and looks acceptable. But later on we will find that this piece was wrong and we have lost time and effort in the process of trying to make the rest of our life pieces fit. It just makes a mess.

So the Holy Spirit is there to guide us—giving us the right pieces (responses), giving us the power of God to face whatever our day holds, and in turn having a different puzzle piece—to give us the peace of God in our lives. In chapter 5 we will look in more depth at the Spirit's role in our life and how to ensure He is in control.

YOUR PERSONAL EVALUATION

We are now ready to look at how to determine what your relationship level with God is.

Put a check mark in the box of all statements with which you agree, or your life is at or beyond that point of commitment.

1. ☐ I have a curiosity about God.

2. ☐ I am certain God exists.*

3. ☐ What I know about God has created a sense of awe in me toward Him.

4. ☐ I acknowledge the authority of God in my life.

5. ☐ I am seeking the truth about God and His existence.

6. ☐ I have decided that I want a relationship with God.*

7. ☐ When I pray, my prayers are usually not centered on my needs and desires.

---

8. ☐ I see God as a personal God, not just a God who started everything and left humans to their own ways.

9. ☐ I have some trust in God.

10. ☐ I am thankful to God for all He has done for me.

11. ☐ Sometimes I feel overwhelmed by my relationship with God.

12. ☐ I have invited Jesus into my life as my Savior and as the Lord of my life.*

13. ☐ I have an inner desire to obey God even if I do not always succeed in doing so.

14. ☐ I am aware of areas in my life that are not pleasing to God.*

15. ☐ I read the Bible and pray.

16. ☐ I pray because I know I should.

17. ☐ I allow the Holy Spirit to control my actions as much as I can.*

18. ☐ I am, or have been, excited about my relationship with God.

---

19. ☐ I am convinced God is on my side.*

20. ☐ I have a hunger for the Word at times.

21. ☐ I try to obey God's Word most of the time.*

22. ☐ I pray because I feel it is spiritually the most healthy thing to do.

23. ☐ I obey God most of the time.*

24. ☐ I trust God in most things.*

25. ☐ I have a strong sense of being a loved child of God.

26. ☐ God is helping me develop more self-control in difficult situations.

27. ☐ I have a healthy sense of my worth in God's eyes.

28. ☐ I feel secure in my relationship with God.

29. ☐ I see God as a good, kind, and loving Father whom I can trust.

---

30. ☐ I obey God out of love rather than fear.

31. ☐ I have a strong desire to please God in all that I do.

32. ☐ I am becoming very submissive to the will of God. I do not struggle as much as I used to.

33. ☐ I understand the Word as I read it.

34. ☐ I have a clear sense of the presence of God in my life and His love and acceptance of me.

35. ☐ I have an intensifying desire to draw closer to God, to trust Him more.

36. ☐ I have surrendered almost every area of my life to the Lord.

37. ☐ I can sense an increase in the intensity and pleasure from my worship and praise of the Lord both publicly and privately.

38. ☐ I find myself praying a lot for things I know God is interested in.

39. ☐ There is an increasing amount of self-control, peace, and joy in my life.

40. ☐ I have a greater feeling of security and confidence in who I am before the Lord.

---

41. ☐ I have a deep love for God and desire to do His will 100 percent of the time, even though I may fall short of that goal.*

42. ☐ I see God stripping away from my life many unnecessary things. This is pleasing to me, and I do not struggle against what He wants to do.*

43. ☐ I desire to please God at all times and never resent His asking me to do anything. I always serve Him from a willing heart.

44. ☐ The Scriptures are alive and meaningful to me.*

45. ☐ Praise and worship are very important in my times with the Lord.*

46. ☐ I attend church not just for the fellowship, but because of my great love for the Lord and my desire to worship Him and learn more about Him.*

47. ☐ If I have to choose between doing something that pleases me and obeying God, I will obey God *almost* every time.*

48. ☐ My faith is such that it would be almost impossible for anyone to be able to undermine it or keep me from following God's will in any given situation.*

49. ☐ I have regular, scheduled times with the Lord. They are very important to me.*

50. ☐ I can see a real difference in my behavior and outlook if I miss even one or two times with the Lord.

51. ☐ I seek always to know and follow the will of God in everything I do, even in what others would consider trivial matters.*

52. ☐ With all my heart, I desire to walk free from sin.

53. ☐ It grieves me when I sin.*

54. ☐ There is rarely or never an instance when I plan to sin (such as thinking about how to deceive or lie to someone, steal, or to "get away" with some act).*

55. ☐ Hearing gossip grieves my spirit.*

56. ☐ I avoid gossiping at all costs.*

57. ☐ I seem to have a real peace in my life no matter what is going on around me. I stay focused on the Lord and not my circumstances.*

58. ☐ I want God to help me remove *every* weakness I have.*

59. ☐ I often get excited when God points out a weakness He wants to deal with because I know that in dealing with it, I will become more like Jesus.

60. ☐ I use praise and worship in times of trouble to express my faith in God and to help me keep my eyes on Him, not the circumstances.

61. ☐ I have a strong conviction that God is in control of all things.*

62. ☐ I have a real sense of God's presence in my life at all times. I talk to Him much of the day.

63. ☐ My conversation with God is not always talking about my needs. Often it includes worship and praise of Him, and expressions of gratefulness for creation and those He has brought into my life.

64. ☐ I do not use prayer as an instrument for getting my way or my desires fulfilled.*

65. ☐ I do not resent it when God chooses to change my plans for the day.*

66. ☐ There is overwhelming awe, joy, and excitement when I think of my relationship with God and how sweet it is.

67. ☐ My relationship with God means everything to me. I try to guard it so nothing can change it or interfere with it.

68. ☐ Thoughts of my relationship with God and/or times of worship can bring tears of joy and gratitude.

69. ☐ I live to please the Lord. I place His desires above my own.

70. ☐ I have joy in surrendering absolutely to every wish of God.

71. ☐ I try to do what God wants immediately rather than procrastinating or trying to find a way around what I know He wants.

72. ☐ I have a strong sense of God's presence and friendship at all times.

73. ☐ I do not withhold anything in my life from the Lord.

74. ☐ I desire to live a morally clean life.

75. ☐ I often have a sense of sin in my life in small areas I know others would not consider important.

76. ☐ Little things that once were overlooked or in which I compromised are no longer tolerated.

77. ☐ I sense God is fine tuning my life, stripping away things that have been a hindrance in my walk with Him.

78. ☐ I find prayer is a constant flow throughout the day, almost as though the Lord were visible beside me.

79. ☐ I pray much less for myself and my own interests than I do for the things I know are on the heart of God.

80. ☐ I try to avoid praying for anything that I do not know is in God's will, and may be just my own desire or wants.

81. ☐ I sense that each of the fruits of the Spirit are present in some degree in my life.

82. ☐ I have a strong desire to live at peace with everyone and do whatever I can to live this way.

83. ☐ I am seen by others as a person of great wisdom and self-control.

84. ☐ People often seek my advice or counsel.

85. ☐ I am an optimistic person.

86. ☐ I do not withhold from God *any* area of my life. He has *carte blanche*.

87. ☐ I have an absolute conviction that God is in control of all things.

88. ☐ I rarely fear anything.

Identifying Your Relationship Level

You are now ready to identify your current level of spiritual growth and relationship with God.

First, go back to the list of questions and make sure the questions with an asterisk have a check on them. If not, identify the first time an asterisk is skipped. Your relationship level will automatically be within that level or lower.

Second, identify the number of checks within each category listed below and write that number in the blank provided. In each category, a designated number of checks is necessary to qualify for the next level. This number should include all asterisked question checked. Find the highest level which meets this criteria and you have identified your current level to begin/continue your spiritual journey.

Holy Sovereign (Questions 1–7) In this category, you should have six checks to advance to the next level. _____

Suffering Savior (Questions 8–18) In this category, you should have nine checks to advance to the next level. _____

Loving Father (Questions 19–29) In this category, you should have nine checks to advance to the next level. _____

Faithful Companion (Questions 30–40) In this category, you should have nine checks to advance to the next level. _____

Good Friend (Questions 41–63) In this category, you should have seventeen checks to advance to the next level. _____

Intimate Friend (Questions 64–88) Because "Intimate Friend" is the last category, there are no numbers for going on to another level. At the end of this step, you will hear, "Well done, good and faithful servant! Come and share your Master's happiness."

Third, once you have identified your current level, go back to the list of statements and identify those items for which you cannot put a check. To draw closer to God, you must work on the issues. One of the best ways to do this is simply to work through each chapter of those areas where there are statements you could not mark. This will help establish the foundation of your relationship with the Lord. If you still are having trouble after that, turn to chapter 9 and go through that material.

If you find you are sporadic in your markings, with some marks in several levels but many missed in those same levels, then go back to basics. Start with chapter 3 (or the first one you find missing more than two in the unit), and work through each action step you realize has yet to be true in your life.

If you repeat or duplicate something already true of you, you will find it will simply serve as a reinforcement of that truth in your life. It is better to repeat than to leave holes in the foundation of faith and trust you are building in the Lord. Actually, we suggest that everyone may find it helpful to read all levels in order to refresh their appreciation of the journey God has already taken them on.

One final note. As you go through the remaining chapters, you will undoubtedly find the Holy Spirit speaking to you about things in your life. The person who wants to benefit most from this material will read with pen and paper near in order to jot down those things He is showing. In this way the reader will be able to remember and interact with His promptings and derive the greatest benefit from the material, thus reaching the goal sooner. Wise persons will respond to the correcting light of the Holy Spirit, for they know He wants the best for them.

PREPARATION ACTION STEP

On a special trip many people like to take notes of what they see and have done so they can remember their experiences in the future. We highly recommend you do the same for your spiritual journey. For maximum benefit we suggest you take the following spiritual journey preparation action step. (Each chapter will use the title of the chapter as the code for the action step. Thus "SJ" stands for "spiritual journey.") This will be helpful in seeing what God is showing you, and even in getting back to the right road if you get sidetracked.

Action Step SJ-1

Start a spiritual journey notebook-journal. It is best if this is a three ring binder with dividers since you will have several sections. Head the first section "Attributes of God," the second section "Emotions/Feelings and Desires," the third section "Prayer Request Record," the fourth section "Lies I Have Believed," the fifth section "Questions I Still Have," and the last section "My Current View of God."

As you come across appropriate material, write it on the corresponding sheet. Where applicable, you may want to write your own thoughts about each new entry.

Begin with the attributes of God. Consider these questions and then, if you wish, write:

- What difference does it make to me that God is _____ ?

- How would it affect my faith if He were not this way?

- What are some ways I have seen this area of His nature in my own experience?

For the Emotions/Feelings and Desires section, If the area is a negative one—like fear, hate, revenge, or unforgiveness—ask:

- Why do I feel/respond this way?

- What are the consequences of feeling/responding this way?
- What does God say about this?
- What reason(s) have I given myself for continuing on in this way? (I am born this way; I am this way because of my family background and how I was mistreated; It's not my fault; The other person deserves this treatment; I can't help myself.)
- What do I sense God wants me to do about this? How can I do that?

When you reach the last question of application, you may want to consider as part of the solution such things as:

- What lies of Satan have I believed?
- Why am I willing to believe that lie rather than God's truth?
- What Scripture verse can I claim to counteract this lie with the truth?

Ask the Holy Spirit to show you what is happening and how to solve the problem. For many, writing down such answers is helpful in seeing the truth.

Note: You can use the above materials to stimulate prayer such as prayers of thanksgiving for who God is and what you have seen Him do, how you have seen Him control your emotions and feelings, ways He has met needs and answered prayers, and thanking Him that He is in the process of changing you in _____ area.

♦

Art Linkletter once saw a little boy drawing a picture. He asked, "What are you drawing?" The boy replied, "A picture of God." Linkletter proceeded to give the child a lesson in theology explaining that no one knows what God looks like. To which the boy confidently responded, "They will when I get done."

You are about to embark on a wonderful journey to clarify in your mind what God is like. Trying to explain God is like trying to explain a kiss. You can check the dictionary definition: " A caress with the lips; a gentle touch or contact." But does that really capture the essence of what a kiss is? Does that describe what a mother does when she tenderly places her lips on the forehead of her newborn child? Is that what the young lover does when he says "good night" to his love?

Just as mere words cannot completely capture all that is involved in what we know by experience and attempt to describe as a "kiss," we also cannot fully comprehend, explain, or define "God." We can, however, know Him through experiencing His revelation of Himself to us in His Word, the Bible, and in the person of Jesus Christ. We can know Him as we see His involvement in our lives in every area we allow Him to touch.

The next six chapters will take you on a journey that brings you closer to God. You have two choices as to how you take it. First, no matter at which level you determined you were, you can begin with chapter 4 and go straight through. Or you can start at your own level (for example, chap. 6 if you are at the Loving Father level) and read from there to the end of the book. We would suggest you take the first option if you have the time and are not too anxious to get into deeper things right away. In this way you will reinforce your current foundation and pick up any pieces that may need strengthening or that are missing. Enjoy your journey!

◆

1. Tim Stafford, *Knowing the Face of God* (Grand Rapids, Mich.: Zondervan), 107.

2. For our purposes we are using the word *trust* to indicate the action that results from the faith in the Lord we have gained from past experiences with Him through the Word as well as in our life.

PART TWO

Levels of Intimacy with God

Chapter 3

Level 1:

Holy Sovereign

For since the creation of the world God's invisible qualities—his eternal power and divine nature—have been clearly seen, being understood from what has been made, so that men are without excuse.

ROMANS 1:20

—

(A Special Note to Our Readers)
We wrote this book with the assumption that most readers already believe in God and have at least a desire to have a personal relationship with Him if they don't already. However, there may be those who would like to feel that way but do not.

We don't want to neglect you, yet space does not allow us to cover everything you need to know. For example, we will not try to cover here how God has spoken to humans through any of the many ways He has chosen to do so throughout history. If by the time you have read chapters 3 and 4 you still are not at the point you believe in God's existence or in the incarnation

—

of Jesus—God living among us in the flesh—then please go to Resource 3 in the back of this book, choose one or more of the starred books, and read it.

You are also invited to contact us at the address given in the "How to Use this Book" section at the beginning of this book. We have a forty-five page 8½x11 booklet which takes you step-by-step through this process of understanding God as Holy Sovereign and Suffering Savior. The cost is five dollars (made out to Dian Ginter) which covers printing, shipping, and handling. Dian is also available to correspond or talk by phone about such questions that may be keeping you from committing fully to God.

◆

She's not breathing!" Imagine these words to be the first you hear at the delivery of your daughter. Glen's wife Nancy had not had a healthy pregnancy. She had coughed and been congested most of the seven months carrying their child.

Their daughter, Kerry, came into the world more than two months early, and she was not breathing. The doctors worked frantically. Nurses set about inserting tubes and IV's. To make matters worse, the nurses were not well trained in this kind of emergency. They were "filling in" because the regular nurses were on strike.

Questions flooded Nancy and Glen's minds: "Lord, why is this happening? Have we done anything wrong to deserve this catastrophe? God, where are You in our deepest time of sorrow and pain?" But in the midst of the pain, the disappointment, and the heartache, Nancy and Glen learned a very significant lesson: God is sovereign.

First, with the nurses on strike, Kerry was transferred to the Neonatal Intensive Care Unit at Loma Linda University, which in 1977 was the premiere neonatal unit in the country. There she would have one doctor and one specialized nurse at her bedside twenty-four hours a day.

Second, this kind of treatment demands extravagant prices. But since the hospital where their daughter was born was unable to provide care due to the strike, the health insurance provider picked up the entire $250,000 bill except for one $15 eye exam.

Third and most important to Glen and Nancy, they learned through the trauma, waiting, and praying to trust the God of the universe in a way that would call Glen into the ministry. Was it coincidence? We think not. This merely reflects the sovereignty of God. In other words, it was a God-incidence, not a coincidence.

Throughout the centuries people have tried to put together a cosmic puzzle without knowing how. For many, their efforts had been further complicated because they realized that even if they succeeded, they had no assurance there was any genuine deity to discover. Furthermore, even if there were, would they like what they saw? This cosmic challenge is the God-puzzle. For ages people have tried to discover if god(s) exists and if so, in what form.

To further complicate the process, the enemy of our souls has secretly slipped into the puzzle boxes many extra pieces which look great, but if used completely distort the true image of God. Too often the picture which results is either so gruesome they reject such a god, or so alluring as to keep the person away from the true God. They use their own experiences and their own humanity to form their understanding of deity, which often ends up being a multitude of either monstrous deities to be feared or ones fashioned in their own image. Thus, they are tricked into believing they have solved the puzzle, when in fact they believe in something that does not even exist.

For example, the Romans and Greeks created gods that were simply oversized editions of themselves with larger than life human flaws. Other cultures, especially tribal, have demon-like deities. Animistic cultures choose to worship nature. Hindu cultures pay homage to over three million deities! Most religions leave humans very unsatisfied and yearning to fill the void they feel, longing to make the pieces fit and to solve the puzzle.

In fact, Pascal, the famous French philosopher, identified this feeling when he said: "There is a God-shaped vacuum in the heart of every man that cannot be filled by anyone except God made known through Jesus Christ." He solved the God-puzzle because he knew where to find the missing pieces.

Indeed, religion is sometimes defined as a human being's best attempt to find God, while Christianity is defined as God's best attempt to find the human being. Unfortunately, even when people have been introduced to the Judeo-Christian God of the Bible, there have too often been some distortions of His being, resulting in wrong perceptions of who God really is and what He is like.

Some see Him as Policeman of the Universe just waiting to pounce on anyone who takes a wrong step. Their God-given conscience makes them feel guilty for wrongdoing, but they fail to see God as a forgiving God. They see Him only as a judging God. Others see just the opposite. To them their deity is a disinterested One who created everything and then withdrew to let mankind do whatever it wishes. Still others see God as permissive, letting mankind do what it wants, never to be punished because they worship a loving, all-forgiving God.

So what is the true picture of God? Well, that is what this book is all about. We will be looking at the accurate picture of God as revealed by God Himself through the Bible. We will be seeing not only what He is like, but how we can have a personal relationship with Him, drawing ever closer to Him in the process.

Since we believe Christianity is the true revelation of God to the human race, let's examine the process that occurs in this search to solve the God-puzzle.

First, the Bible says in Romans 1:18–20 that God has chosen to reveal Himself to us both *internally* through our conscience, and *externally* through nature. In our first steps toward God, we discover certain broad things about Him.

Seeking the Holy Sovereign

It is interesting to note that the first book of the Bible, Genesis, does not start out trying to prove the existence of God. It states that as a fact in verse 1: "In the beginning God created. . . ." Much later, in the New Testament, Romans 1:19–21 sheds a light on why God did not try to convince us He exists. Paul said that "what may be known about God is plain to them, because God has made it plain to them. For since the creation of the world God's invisible qualities—his eternal power and divine nature—have been clearly seen, being understood from what has been made, so that men are without excuse. For although they knew God, they neither glorified him as God nor gave thanks to him, but their thinking became futile and their foolish hearts were darkened." God has given us both an internal and external witness that He exists. *And* He holds us responsible for rightly responding to that knowledge and desiring to know Him.

Dian lived in India as a missionary from 1969 to 1971. During her time there she heard many stories of people from non-Christian backgrounds who had wanted to know about God and yet, seemed to have had little or no chance to hear. Time after time she heard of a special act on His part: those who had dreams or went into a book store and saw a picture of Jesus, which set off a set of circumstances in which they eventually found Him as their Savior.

The most memorable was a man who lived in the depths of the Indian jungle, far away from any contact with civilization. Villagers there live and die without ever seeing anyone from the outside. This particular man was helping construct a roof. As he looked around from his vantage point, his heart once again longed to know how everything got started. He had heard there was civilization, but he had never seen it. Later he reported that he had a strange compulsion to leave his job and walk away from his village, searching for the answer to "How did everything come to be as it is now?"

He walked for days and suddenly felt he should stop at one particular home. He did and knocked on the door. When he asked his question of the one who answered the door, he was delighted to hear the man respond, "Please come in. I can indeed tell you how everything came to be as it is now."

This villager's longing to know about God, even though he hardly knew how to conceptualize the question, was satisfied that day as this missionary told him of a God who loved him so much He chose to come to earth to rescue him from being separated forever from Him. As the missionary told the man about Jesus, the man understood and invited Him into his life.

One of the things that has always been so special to Dian about this true story is that at that time there were probably much more than half a billion people living in India. And at the same time there were only 1,500 foreign missionaries. Apart from the faithfulness of God, there were few chances this man would even leave his village, let alone stop at probably the only house in the area where someone knew the answer to his question. God alone is the answer for this story. God showed Himself to this man because he was seeking to know the truth.

What Dian heard in India can be repeated by those from Africa, China, and the Middle East—from even here in the Western world. God shows Himself to those who truly, without strings, want to know Him. In fact, He says as much in Jeremiah 29:13 when He says, "You will seek me and find me when you seek me with all your heart."

There are those who seek for God in their own way. Still others refuse the idea of God. Psalm 14:1 tells us of a fool, who says in his heart, "There is no God." He is an oddity because the Bible says nothing about atheists. But even he is not an atheist, as we understand and interpret the term.

The only atheism the Bible knows is not speculative, but practical. By this we mean that if God has no real impact in a person's life, if there are no tangible ways to record His impact in the world, and if He seemingly is not active, then, that person concludes "there must be no God." What do you do if you are wrestling with these kinds of issues in your life?

What steps can you take to sense the presence of a sovereign God in the universe? In the following pages are some action steps on this journey of getting to know if there is a God and then who that God is.

So first stop and think for a minute. What if there is a God and He has all power and all knowledge including knowledge of the future? Does it not make sense that, if He holds mankind responsible for something, in order to be just He will need to communicate to them what it is He wants them to do. Of course, this would mean that such a God would also be capable of communicating with us in a way that we can understand and accept that it comes from Him.

It would also be good if He were not capricious (as the Roman and Greek gods were), and also was good (as opposed to the deities of many cultures). Because He would know the future, He would also know that there would be a multitude of writings, all claiming to be from Him. So again, it would seem logical that a God who desires to tell us something should put it in such a form as to be unquestionably identified as being from Him. With this criteria in mind, look at the Bible and see if it can pass the test.

Action Step HS-1

Pray either of the following prayers or one in your own words expressing your doubts about the existence of God. Remember, if He does not exist, you have not lost anything by praying this prayer. But if He does, you have everything to gain.

God,
I want to know You, if indeed You do exist. At this point I really don't know, but I do want to know the truth. Please show me what is truth and in turn what You expect of me.

Or the following may be closer to your feelings:

> *God,*
> *I know You exist, but I really don't feel at this time that I
> can trust You enough to turn my life over to Your control.
> There are so many questions I have, so many doubts and
> fears. But I want to be able to trust You and to know You
> as I see others know You in a personal way. So I give You
> permission to help me overcome my hesitations so I can
> know and trust You.*

THE RELIABILITY OF THE BIBLE

One question which will inevitably need answering is, "Who wrote the Bible?" The answer lies in the fact that God commissioned both the Old Testament writers (of the first thirty-nine books in the Bible) and the New Testament writers (of the remaining twenty-seven books in the Bible) to write the Word of God in God's own words.

For instance, a prophet by the name of Jeremiah once wrote in Jeremiah 1:4–5,9, "The word of the LORD came to me, saying, 'Before I formed you in the womb I knew you, before you were born I set you apart; I appointed you as a prophet to the nations.' . . . Then the LORD reached out his hand and touched my mouth and said to me, 'Now, I have put my words in your mouth.'"

In the New Testament, one writer whose book depicted events of the end of the earth wrote, "On the Lord's Day I was in the Spirit, and I heard behind me a loud voice like a trumpet, which said: 'Write on a scroll what you see and send it to the seven churches: to Ephesus, Smyrna, Pergamum, Thyatira, Sardis, Philadelphia and Laodicea'" (Rev. 1:10–11). All the Bible writers provide evidence that what they would share with mankind was from God.

If you desire to have a right relationship with God, the Bible is essential because it is God's revelation of Himself to us. Many excellent biblical illustrations show just that. It is through the Bible that you learn how to have a right relationship with God.

However, as we have mentioned, we do not have the space here to defend all aspects of Christianity. So if you have questions about the source and accuracy of the Bible, we can point you in the right direction and can also help you on a personal basis if you still have questions which are unresolved. If you are still uncertain about the reliability of the Scriptures, complete the following optional action step.

Optional Action Step: Read one or more of the following books:
- Gleason L. Archer, *Encyclopedia of Bible Difficulties* (Chicago: Moody Press: 1964).
- Stephen T. Davis, *The Debate About the Bible* (Philadelphia, Pa.: The Westminster Press, 1977).
- Harold Lindsell, *The Bible in the Balance* (Grand Rapids, Mich.: Zondervan, 1979).
- *The Bible: Breathed from God* (Wheaton, Ill.: Victor Books, 1978).
- Charles C. Ryrie, *A Survey of Bible Doctrine* (Chicago: Moody Press, 1972).
- Clifford A. Wilson, *Rocks, Relics and Biblical Reliability* (Grand Rapids, Mich.: Zondervan, 1977).
- F. F. Bruce, *New Testament History* (New York, N.Y.: Doubleday: 1971).
- Josh McDowell, *Evidence That Demands a Verdict* (San Bernardino, Calif.: Here's Life Publishers, 1979).
- John MacArthur, Jr., *Why I Trust the Bible* (Wheaton, Ill.: Victor Books: 1983).
- T. C. Hammond, *In Understanding Be Men* (InterVarsity Press, 1968; rep. 1991, Leicester, England: Cox & Wyman Limited, Reading Berks).
- Philip Wesley Comfort, ed., *The Origin of the Bible* (Wheaton, Ill.: Tyndale House Publishers, 1992).

WHAT IS GOD LIKE?

Often looking at another's character helps us evaluate whether or not we want to get to know that person. God reveals many aspects of His nature to us in the Scriptures.

On the journey of getting to know God, ten of His attributes, which are characteristic or qualities, are usually the most important ones a person at this level will consider: *exists, eternal, Creator, all-powerful, all-knowing, present everywhere, wise, holy, majestic, King.*

The Scriptures clearly show throughout that God is the One and only God. He says He knows of no other.[1] It also shows Him to have no beginning or end and therefore is eternal.[2] God says that He is Creator of everything that exists,[3] has all power,[4] is present everywhere,[5] and has all knowledge which He uses with wisdom.[6] In addition the Bible declares Him to be holy and just,[7] majestic,[8] and King of all.[9] These are very strong claims. If they are true, then what difference does this make in your life?

Action Step HS-2

Evaluate your current belief about God by circling any of the above ten attributes you do not believe about God or still doubt. It might be helpful to list on a sheet of paper the reasons why you reject such an idea as being true. (We will look at those in action step HS-4.) Then turn to resource 1 for Scriptures and suggested readings to help you understand and accept that God in fact does have this attribute or quality. Then, pray what is given at the beginning of that resource.

Although it is not essential you believe God has every one of these attributes before going on, you will probably get more out of the material which follows if you do. If, however, you come to an impasse and cannot fully accept one or more of the qualities about God, you may want to use a prayer similar to the following, making certain you mean what you say. God will not be offended at your honesty. He already knows what you are thinking, but He desires to have you put it into words. You may use this prayer for any hindrance or questions you have.

God,
I still can't understand or accept that You are _____.
So I am choosing to set this aside for now while I look into other aspects about You. I really want to know the truth about You, so I'm asking You to help me answer my questions and remove whatever other blocks may be keeping me from the truth.

Action Step HS-3

Think about the following and answer the questions. God says He is the Creator of all things. If this is true, then what difference does that make in your life? Do you have any responsibility or obligation to Him? What about obedience? Should you obey Him if He created you?

Optional Action Step. In order to understand better His attributes and how they affect you, ask yourself each of the other suggested interaction questions listed in resource 1 concerning God's attributes (nature). Write down your responses and carefully consider what this means to you.

Action Step HS-4

List the limitations you place on God because of your unbelief. Psalm 78 gives an important characteristic of the people of Israel which can also be a warning to us. Psalm 78:21–22 says, "When the LORD heard them, he was very angry; his fire broke out against Jacob, and his wrath rose against Israel, for they did not believe in God or trust in his deliverance."

Why did this happen? They had seen firsthand the work of God delivering them from slavery and meeting their day-to-day needs. Yet they did not believe God. They still questioned His ability and purpose and thus limited God's influence in their lives. Unbelief is a characteristic of many people, both in the Bible and today's world.

Action Step HS-5

Read the Book of Psalms. Record on separate pages in your notebook, under the Attribute section, each attribute or characteristic you observe. If appropriate, note your response to this information and how you have observed this attribute at work in your own experiences either now or in the past.

Action Step HS-6

Examine the evidence for God's existence. The Bible records the experiences of a man named Paul whom God directed to start churches throughout a region known as Asia Minor. He went through a variety of trials and tribulations throughout his life.

One occasion found Paul a prisoner on his way to Rome to stand trial before Nero, who was known for his hatred of Christians. Suddenly a storm arose, threatening the safety of the ship and all on board. As the raging waves of the Mediterranean engulfed them, Paul confidently stated, "But now I urge you to keep up your courage, because not one of you will be lost; only the ship will be destroyed. Last night an angel of the God whose I am and whom I serve stood beside me and said, 'Do not be afraid, Paul. You must stand trial before Caesar; and God has graciously given you the lives of all who sail with you.' So keep up your courage, men, for I have faith in God that it will happen just as he told me" (Acts 27:22–25).

Did you catch his words? "I have faith in God"—a simple yet profound statement of faith expressing a genuine confidence in a living God. Paul's calmness and tranquillity in the middle of turbulence were grounded in a personal knowledge that God was there and in control.

Many today profess to know about God but have never experienced Him in a personal way. There are some who would try to give the impression that a highly educated person cannot believe in God. This is simply not true. Some of the finest doctors and scientists of our day have no trouble believing God is in ultimate control.

Dr. Henry M. Morris, Ph.D., the director of the Institute for Creation Research, has written numerous scholarly books and articles supporting a worldwide flood, creationism, and rebuttals against evolution. Sir William Ramsey, an eminent authority on the geography and history of Asia Minor, once called the Book of Acts in the Bible, "A highly imaginative and carefully colored account of primitive Christianity."[10] After intense investigation, however, he wrote, *The Bearing of Recent Discoveries on the Trustworthiness of the New Testament* in defense of the Bible. His careful study revealed that the Bible is to be trusted not criticized. Pascal, the French philosopher, wrote, "The evidence of God's existence and His gift is more than compelling, but those who insist that they have no need of Him or it, will always find ways to discount the offer."[11]

Now that you have worked through the various action steps of level 1, you should be ready to go to level 2. In order to do so, you need to believe at least the following:

- God exists.

- He is holy, perfect, eternal, all-powerful, present everywhere.

- He has certain requirements of me and I have a responsibility of some kind to Him.

If you can go on, congratulations. You are ready to go to level 2, which is discussed in chapter 5. If not, then take the next step until you can.

Special Action Step: Using the model prayer below as a guide, offer up to God your own prayer which expresses your heart's desire.

Dear God,
Well, here I am again. I still have the following problems
in understanding what is true about You. (List questions,
reservations, areas you do not accept, etc.) *Please show*
me what to do to get over these blocks. Show me any lies I
have been believing. Open my understanding so I can know
and accept the truth.

We then suggest you go to resource 2 and read some of the
suggested materials there and go through the verses given. Note
that you do not have to have *every* single hesitation answered,
only those which keep you from accepting the above marked
areas. Hang in there. God is faithful. He will show you the truth
as you allow Him to teach you about Himself.

♦

1. Deuteronomy 4:35; 32:12; Isaiah 43:10; 44:6.

2. Genesis 21:33; Romans 16:26; Revelation 1:8, 17–18; 21:6,13.

3. Isaiah 44:24.

4. Job 42:2; Revelation 19:6; 21:22.

5. Psalm 139:7–10; Ephesians 1:23.

6. Job 12:13; 36:4; Proverbs 3:19.

7. Joshua 24:19; Daniel 9:14; Isaiah 45:21; Zephaniah 3:5.

8. Isaiah 26:10; Hebrews 1:3.

9. 1 Timothy 6:15.

10. Robert W. Faid, *A Scientific Approach to Christianity* (Green Forest, Ariz.: New Leaf Press, 1990), 13.

11. Pascal, Blaise, *Pensee's* no. 430, translated by H. F. Stewart (New York: Random House, n. d.) as quoted in McDowell, *Evidence That Demands a Verdict*, 12.

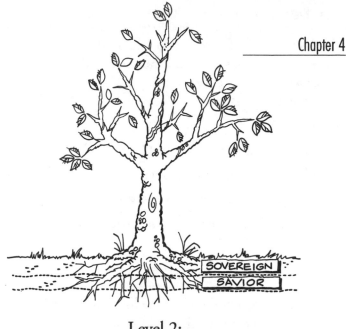

Chapter 4

Level 2:

Sacrificial Savior

For God so loved the world that he gave his one and only son, that whoever believes in him shall not perish but have eternal life.

JOHN 3:16

*T*he seed germinated and new life has begun. The soil in level 1 was fertile, and the roots are now pushing deeper to the second level. God has been accepted as Sovereign, and now we are growing in the knowledge of Christ as our Savior. Beginning with level 2, each chapter will start with one or more action steps you should be doing while reading the chapter.

Action Step SS-1

Start reading the Gospel of John. This fourth book of the New Testament was written by the disciple who was closer to Jesus than any of the others—John. He had an intimate relationship with Jesus and was known as the "beloved disciple." As you read this book, write down in your notebook what you learn about Jesus. Use a separate page with the heading "Jesus" and consider the following questions:

- Who is He?
- What is His relationship to God?
- What type of person was He?
- What kind of things did He say about Himself?
- Why did He come to live on earth?

Action Step SS-2.

Turn to resource 1 and look at the list of nine attributes of God for level 2. Make a page in your journal under "attributes" for each one. Then as you read the Book of John, list those verses that show you this side of God's nature. Remember, Jesus is God. We will be looking at that in this chapter.

The cover article in *U.S. News and World Report* on December 20, 1993, reflected an important question with which millions of people throughout the world have wrestled. Author Jeffrey L. Sheler wrote:

> Today, as in his own time, Jesus of Nazareth remains one of history's most intriguing and enigmatic figures. The religion founded on his teachings counts nearly a third of the world's population as members, yet his words and deeds and the meaning of his life, death and resurrection are subjects of intense debate and sometimes surprising interpretations. Many still ask the question of the ages: "Who is Jesus?[1]

If God is to be known by human beings, it will be on God's terms and in God's chosen way. He took the initiative because finite mankind cannot fully comprehend the nature of an all-powerful, all-knowing, compassionate, and yet forgiving God. And God has chosen to communicate by His Word, the Bible.

It is important to read this primary, reliable revelation God has given to us of Himself. This is why God has so carefully let us know that the Bible is His only written revelation of Himself. (See the bibliography in the resources for books that go into this subject in depth.)

The Bible gives us a very broad, accurate picture of the God of the Universe. Through it God lets humanity know all that is needed in order for people to do what He wants and to live their lives according to His purposes. But as with any picture, especially one made up of individual pieces as a puzzle would be, it is important to have all the pieces in the right place in order to have an accurate picture when you finish. To do that, God took another step so His revelation could be complete.

GOD'S GREATEST REVELATION TO MAN

"God is love." declares John, the beloved friend and disciple of Jesus (1 John 4:16). Throughout the Scriptures, we see the great love of God for mankind. His love is unchanging, unending, unconditional. In Jeremiah 31:3 He says to us, "I have loved you with an everlasting love; I have drawn you with loving-kindness." God initiates. He loves us first and we in turn need to respond to His love.

God wants to show His love and His graciousness to us. Isaiah presented a beautiful picture of how the Creator God of the universe longs to have us in His presence. It described Him sitting on His throne, as though looking out over the crowd for us. When He sees us, He rises to greet us—a sign of great honor—that Holy God would rise when we come into His presence. "And therefore the Lord [earnestly] waits [expectant, looking and longing] to be gracious to you, and therefore He lifts Himself up, that He may have mercy on you and show loving-kindness to you" (Isa. 30:18, AMP).

What an awesome thought! The great God who has the whole universe to take up His attention not only knows I exist, but He looks for me and honors me when He sees me. How can that be? You may be saying, "This may be true for some people, but certainly it is not true of me. You don't know all I've done, all I've been. God might accept me, but He surely would not long to be with me."

In fact, this is true of anyone who is willing to take the necessary steps to come into a right relationship with God. God's love makes it possible. Anyone who has ever lived has sinned enough to stay permanently separated from God. In fact, God Himself knew we could never come into His presence through our own efforts.

This set up a dilemma only He could solve. And solve it He did. The Bible says in John 3:16, "For God so loved the world that he gave his one and only Son, that whoever believes in him shall not perish but have eternal life."

God chose to become human in the person of Jesus while still maintaining His deity. In this way Jesus could live a fully perfect life and earn the right—through the shedding of His own blood when He was killed—to be a substitute for our sin. We will see in a moment how God loves us so much that He intervenes in this otherwise hopeless situation and gives us a free, yet costly gift of spiritual life.

However, when one chooses not to accept God's only provision for our sins—the free gift God offers which allows us to live with Him forever—the consequences are our responsibility, not God's. He has reached out to us in love; He has done all that it takes to secure our unending life with Him. But in the final analysis, the decision of one's eternal destiny rests in each individual's hand: Will each accept the free offer of salvation—the ONLY way salvation can come—or instead choose to reject it and try a way doomed to failure?

We have to come on God's terms, but His terms are bathed in a loving heart that wants the very best for us. But we are not able to know God until we are introduced to Him by Jesus. Only Jesus has the ability to make this introduction because only He took care of the sin that made us spiritually dead and in essence enemies of God.[2]

Jesus, who is very God Himself, the second person of the Trinity,[3] is so in love with you that He has chosen you to be His for eternity. So He did what was necessary to "clean you up" and let you live in heaven forever. All you have to do is to accept what He has done for you and ask to be His for eternity.

Some have described this process as one of crossing a unique bridge. The bridge, provided by God, spans an otherwise impossible distance between us as sinners and a holy, just God. Anyone desiring to reach Him must first cross over the gulf by the only way provided.

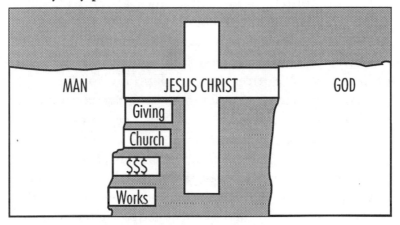

Strewn along the bank of the gorge are the numerous unsuccessful man-made inventions which have been used to try to cross the gap. Two of the most popular are the path of good works and the road of religious activity. All were constructed by human beings according to their own ideas about how God should be reached. But God's evaluation of them comes in Proverbs 14:12: "There is a way that seems right to a man, but in the end it leads to death."

Jesus put it very clearly when asked how one goes about getting to heaven. He replied, "I am the way and the truth and the life. No one comes to the Father except through me" (John 14: 6).

This is a bold statement, which if not true, makes Jesus a liar and definitely not God. What arrogance, conceit, and pride it would be to say you alone are the way to God, if in fact there were many other ways. And the Bible says God hates pride;[4] therefore, if Jesus is proud, He could not be God.

But He *is* God, claimed to be so,[5] and His life proved He was.[6] It was sinless.[7] This is why He could die for us. He was perfect and became a perfect substitute for us by dying in our place. This is why He becomes the firm, stable bridge to God, why He alone can introduce us to God, why He alone is the only way to God. The cost was great—His very life—but to Him it was worth it. He loved us so much, and we have only to accept what He has done on our behalf in order to receive all the benefits of being connected rightly with Him. So the question is how does one cross over the bridge through Jesus in order to establish a personal relationship with God?

Probably some people reading this book have yet to establish such a personal relationship with God. They know all about Him, may have even asked Him to be with them or to help them. They most likely have confessed many of their sins and asked for forgiveness. But they have never asked Him to come *into* their life, to forgive all their sins, and to *take control* of their life so He can make them the kind of person He wants them to be. They have asked God for companionship and guidance but never relationship. They have strongly desired His help, but not His control no matter how lovingly it is given.

There are other people who feel they need to clean up their life before coming to God or do good works or otherwise earn their right to be with Him. This is not possible. It would be like taking a filthy dirty rag and trying to clean a muddy windshield. That is why Jesus died for us while we were still sinners.[8] He paid for *all* our sins, from the time of our birth until our last breath on earth.[9] All we have to do is to accept the free gift of salvation that is offered through Jesus Christ to anyone who wants it. [10]

Action Step SS-3

If you would now like to begin having a personal relationship with God, check each box that accurately reflects your feelings.

- ☐ I believe God is good and wants the best for me.
- ☐ I am a sinner.
- ☐ I recognize my sins are keeping me from God.
- ☐ I cannot get rid of my sin on my own.
- ☐ I want to be free from my sin.
- ☐ I want to have a right relationship with God.
- ☐ I believe that Jesus died and paid for my sins.
- ☐ God has a right to be in control of my life.
- ☐ I want to give God control of every area in my life because I trust Him.

Now go to action step SS-4a or 4b.

Action Step SS-4a

If you have not been able to agree with each of these statements, pray whichever of the following that best expresses your heart.

Dear God,

I do not understand fully how to have a personal relationship with You, but I want to. I understand that I must learn about Your Son, Jesus, and what He did for me. Help me understand all I need to know about Him. Help me learn more about You and how to establish a good relationship with You. Open my understanding. Remove anything that is keeping me from You.

Or if you are already past the point above:

Dear God,

I am just beginning to learn about Jesus and Who He really is—actually God living here on earth to serve as an example for me and to die for my sins. I still have some questions that need to be answered before I can make any commitment of my life to You. Please help me find the answers.

Or if you are already past the point above:

Dear God,

I know a lot about Jesus, but I have never taken the step of inviting Him into my life as my Savior and Lord. Help me to be able to surrender my will to You so I can take this life-changing step.

Optional Action Step: (For those still having reservations.). At this point you will want to list whatever reservations are keeping you from inviting Him into your life.

Go back and look at the attributes and the material you have already studied along with other attributes listed in resource 1. You can also look in resource 2 for suggestions on solutions to your reservations.

Action Step SS-4b

If you have been able to agree with each one of these statements, then read the following prayer. If it reflects what is in your heart, express it to God. Believe that God will answer your prayer of invitation.[11]

Jesus tells us in Revelation 3:20 that this is exactly what He wants to do: "Behold, I stand at the door [of your life], and knock: if any man hear my voice, and open the door [invites Him to come in], I will come in to him, and will sup with him [have fellowship]" (KJV, words of explanation added).

Holy God,

I want to know You so much, yet I know my sin has kept me from doing so. I believe You came to earth in the person of Jesus to die on the cross in my place so I could go to heaven. I now want to ask Jesus to come into my life, to forgive my sins, and to make me the kind of person You want me to be. I do not knowingly withhold any area of my life from You. Thank You for making it possible to be in a right relationship with You. Help me to know how to walk with You step by step. In Jesus' name, Amen.

Action Step SS-5

Now that you have established a relationship with God, you will want to start charting your growth. Turn to resource 4 and either fill out the chart or preferably make one to keep in your journal. At each new level you will be coming back to the chart, marking your progress. The important thing is to be honest. Ask God to help you determine what is true. If you use the same standard for all future markings, you will have a consistent tool for evaluating growth.

GROWTH IS IMPORTANT

Now that you are in a right relationship with God, you have a spiritual life. So just as you have to eat physically in order to grow, so you will need nourishment to develop your new spiritual life.

Action Step SS-6

Develop practices for a healthy, daily walk with the Lord. Now that you have the life of God within you—people call it being born again—you will want to grow in your spiritual life. This is extremely important, as important as eating is to physical life. Dian shares an easy way Campus Crusade teaches about growing in the Lord. They use a simple acrostic of G.R.O.W.T.H. which uses the first letter of each word in the process.

Go to God daily in prayer.[12] Prayer is simply talking to God: telling Him what is on our hearts, confiding in Him, relying on Him, listening to Him speak to our hearts.

One important way to listen is to: **R**ead God's Word/Instruction Manual/Love Letter—the Bible.[13] As we saw in chapter 3 (review this), the Bible is unique and comes straight from the heart of God to us. Among other things, it is designed by our Creator to show us how to live life successfully, how to know exactly what He wants from us, and in turn what He wants to do for us. It shows us how to overcome all the many problems we will face and how to be all He created us to be.

As we read God's Word and pray, He will let us know what He wants us to do. We need to: **O**bey what He shows us to do.[14] This means not 50 percent, 75 percent, or even 99 percent. It means 100 percent commitment to obedience. This we can do when we follow the "H" of GROWTH, which will be discussed below.

Witnessing or sharing with others what Jesus has done for you becomes a natural thing to do as you start to grow.[15] You have discovered something wonderful, are falling in love with the Creator of the universe, and want to share it with everyone. The wise person will do this with discretion, asking God to show when and where to speak and depending on Him for the right words to share.

A key part of growth is **T**rusting God with every aspect of our lives.[16] This means having faith in what God says, believing it, and then applying it in whatever situation we are facing. Trust is the result, the action that occurs, when we have faith in God. Without the other elements in Growth, trust will not develop and whatever trust we have can be weakened by lack of spiritual growth. There is a strong correlation between each of the elements of Growth.

Finally we reach the central element of Growth—the **H**oly Spirit. We need to draw on His power in order to live success-fully the Christian life.[17] This is a simple process, yet one most believers fail to grasp. To fail to do this dooms you to a mediocre Christian life. To walk daily in His power is to prepare yourself to draw closer in a genuine and deep way without the distrac-tions that too often come in many believer's lives.

Charles Swindoll describes the Holy Spirit's importance in the believer's life in this way:

> It is possible to be converted and yet not live on a spiritual plane. It is one thing to become a Christian. It is another

thing entirely to become a Spirit-filled Christian. The tragedy is that so many are converted and so few Spirit-filled. When this happens, a person misses the best God has to offer us on earth.

What fuel is to a car, the Holy Spirit is to the believer. He energizes us to stay the course. He motivates us in spite of the obstacles. He keeps us going when the road gets rough. It is the Spirit who comforts us in our distress, who calms us in times of calamity, who becomes our companion in loneliness and grief, who spurs our "intuition" into action, who fills our minds with discernment when we are uneasy about a certain decision. In short, He is our spiritual fuel. When we attempt to operate without Him or to use some substitute fuel, all systems grind to a halt.[18]

In a nutshell, here is how the Holy Spirit works in our lives.

First, understand that the Holy Spirit comes to live within the Christian at the time of spiritual birth.[19] From that moment forward the Christian is indwelt by the Spirit, but not necessarily filled.[20] God gives us the free will to decide how much of our lives the Spirit is allowed to control. To be walking as He wants us to, He need to be 100 percent in control. Ninety-nine percent yielded to Him means we are 100 percent in control in His eyes. He calls this being "carnal"[21] which means we are following the desires of our flesh, not His Spirit.

Second, recognize that the Holy Spirit is the source of power for everything the Christian does.[22] This includes the things we are capable of doing as well as those things where we are weak. Only when we let Him be in control in all areas are we truly able to experience the abundant and full life God intends for each Christian to have.[23]

Third, we allow the Holy Spirit to guide and direct us by letting Jesus be in control in our lives.[24]

Fourth, we seek to be filled with the Spirit. This can be done by recognizing that we have been in control of our lives, repenting of our self-control, and asking the Holy Spirit to once again take control of our lives and help us become all God intends for us.

Once you have done this, you need to keep short accounts with God by confessing all sin as soon as it happens or as soon as the Spirit shows you something that God wants to change. If you get in control of your life again, then confess that, and ask the Spirit once more to take control of your life.[25] You will also want to ask Him to show you why you chose to take control again and what you need to do to avoid that next time. Many people call this "spiritual breathing" where you exhale the impure and inhale the pure.

You will greatly benefit from reading each of the verses in the footnotes of this chapter and making this process a part of your daily walk. We would also recommend your reading the small booklet, "Have You Made the Wonderful Discovery of the Spirit-filled Life?"[26] as well as the book by Bill Bright, *The Holy Spirit: The Key to Supernatural Living.*[27] Two other great classics are *Baptism & Fullness* by John R. W. Stott,[28] and *The Holy Spirit* by John Walvoord.[29]

If you do not already attend a good church where the Bible is taught and God is honored, you need to ask the Lord to show you where He wants you to worship. This is such an important thing for all believers to do, that it will be discussed further in chapter 10.

Action Step SS-6b

Now that you have the very life of God in you, you will want to add some other important things to the elements for GROWTH. These will help you stay spiritually healthy and add to your growth potential.

Quiet Times: Use the two formats in resource 9A, "Today's Quiet Time Summary," and resource 9B, "Area to Work On," to help you keep track of what God is showing you and for accountability. Keep these in your notebook.

Important Things to Remember (and to say out loud whenever Satan tries to make me doubt these truths)

- God will never forsake me no matter what (Heb. 13:5).
- I am special to God. He accepts me just as I am. He delights in me. (Isa. 30:18; Jer. 29:14; Ps. 37:23; Zeph. 3:17).
- God loves me unconditionally and eternally (Rom. 8:38).

Important Things to Do

- Express my love for God often.
- Thank the Lord for my relationship with Him.
- Thank the Lord for what He is teaching me about Himself.
- Praise and worship the Lord in songs and words.
- Be aware of enemy temptations and resist them.
- When problems come and I feel depressed, remind myself that at least God loves me and I am special to Him. Remind myself that He has not lost control and will make this work together for good according to His promise in Romans 8:28. Therefore I can thank Him for them (1 Thess. 5:18).

How to Recognize and Resist Enemy Attacks

- Anything that attacks or tries to undermine the nature or goodness of God in my eyes; mistrust or questioning of God's goodness, power, and love.
- Anything that tries to interfere in my relationship with God or that tries to become more important in my life than He is. (This includes family members, job, etc.)
- Anything violating or questioning the things in the Bible or trying to undermine my confidence in it.
- Lies such as "Your sins are not fully forgiven" or "You've done wrong things that can never be forgiven no matter how many times you confess them."
- Fear; this is always from Satan, not God (1 Tim. 1:7).

- Negative thoughts about others; Satan is the accuser of the brethren.

Action Step SS-7

Open a new section in your journal entitled "Benefits of My Life in God." Write down the benefits you have observed and understand are true in your new life in Jesus. Consider what difference it makes to realize that God greatly loves you and cares about everything that happens to you. Give specific examples when possible. Then thank God for these things. Update it each time God shows you more benefits.

Action Step SS-8

Although we do not base our knowledge of what is true in our lives solely on our feelings, under normal circumstances feelings will come when we are obedient to God. If appropriate, write down in your notebook how you feel about yourself now versus before you invited Jesus into your life. Less guilt? Cleaner? More peace? More assurance about your eternal destiny? Joy? If you are not experiencing one or more of these, ask the Lord to help you start feeling them. But be careful not to base your confidence on your feelings. Only base them on what God says is true about you in His Word.

Now you have crossed over from spiritual death and no relationship with God into having His life—eternal life—in you, and being His child. You should be ready to go on to level 3 and the Loving Father.

Action Step SS-9

To make certain this is true, go back to the quiz in chapter 2 and verify that you can answer all the questions necessary to start level 3. This is a wonderful level, as You get to know God the

Father in a more personal, loving way than in level 1 or 2. Naturally as you draw closer to Him—and especially because He now is your Father, your perfect heavenly Father—special quality and depth in your relationship should develop. Anticipate this developing relationship with all members of the Godhead as you would the most wonderful meal, the greatest of vacations—whatever it is that brings anticipation.

◆

1. Jeffrey L. Sheler, "Who Was Jesus?," *U.S. News and World Report* (December 20, 1993), 58–62.

2. For further reading on this, see Romans 5.

3. For a good book explaining the Trinity read chapter 2 of *Essential Christianity*, by Dr. Walter Martin (Ventura, Calif.: Regal Books, 1962).

4. Proverbs 6:16–18.

5. John 10:30; 14:8–11.

6. John 20:28, 31; Matthew 27:54.

7. John 8:46.

8. Romans 5:8; 1 John 4:10.

9. 1 John 2:2.

10. John 3:15–16.

11. 1 John 5:14–15.

12. John 15:7.

13. Acts 17:11.

14. John 14:21.

15. Matthew 4:19; John 15:8.

16. 1 Peter 5:7.

17. Galatians 5:16–17; Acts 1:8.

18. Charles R. Swindoll, *Flying Closer to the Flame* (Dallas, Tex.: Word Publishers, 1993), 75.

19. John 14:16–17, 23.

20. Ephesians 5:18.

21. 1 Corinthians. 3:1–3.

22. John 7:37–39.

23. John 10:10.

24. John 15.

25. 1 John 1:9.

26. Copywritten 1966 by Campus Crusade for Christ.

27. Bill Bright, *The Holy Spirit: Key to Supernatural Living* (Orlando, Fla.: New Life Publications, 1980).

28. John R. W. Stott, *Baptism & Fullness: The Work of the Holy Spirit Today* (Downers Grove, Ill.: InterVarsity Press, 1964).

29. John F. Walvoord, *The Holy Spirit* (Findlay, Ohio: Dunham Publishing Company, 1958).

Chapter 5

SOVEREIGN
SAVIOR
FATHER

Level 3:
Loving Father

I will be a Father to you, and you will be my sons and daughters, says the Lord Almighty.

2 CORINTHIANS 6:18

*W*e are about to begin a wonderful section of this study. It goes beyond salvation and into what can become the closest of relationships with God. It would be difficult to find a religion apart from Judeo-Christianity that presents God as good, kind, and loving—one who wants to help His creation, not just rule them. More of His loving heart will be revealed in this section.

Action Step LF-1

Start reading 1 John. This small book tells a lot about the love of God. As you read it, write in your journal, on a separate page, a description of God's love as you see it described here. Keep adding to the previous journal pages those things you find that are appropriate. Put beside them any comments or observations or ways you can apply it to your own life.

Action Step LF-2

Write out your understanding right now of who God is as a Father. Do you have any reservations or questions? You will find it helpful to identify how these questions interfere with your current relationship with Him and in drawing closer to God. Let God show you the truth in these areas as you work through this section. Write the truth when you find it next to the misunderstandings.

Action Step LF-3

Create a separate page for your notebook with the heading "Father." On that page write down what positive things you learn about God the Father and His nature. Then, if you do not feel this way about Him, write in pencil under the positive statement what your current view is. If possible, identify why you feel this way. Ask the Lord to show you the source: a negative experience, unanswered prayer, or a negative authority figure such as a parent that has caused you to look at the Father in a wrong way. Then ask Him to help you change your under-standing of Him to line up with the truth and to make your feelings respond positively, too. Later, when you no longer have this wrong response, you can mark in red ink, "Now I believe the truth."

Action Step LF-4

Turn to resource 1 and look at the list of God's attributes as a Loving Father. Make a page for each attribute in your notebook under "Attributes." Then, as you read 1 John or any other

Scriptures, write down those verses that show you this side of God's nature. Answer the attribute interaction questions.

♦

When Jesus Christ walked this planet, He blew away everything clouding the typical perception of what God was like. God is no longer to be seen as an impersonal force ruling creation. He is not a tyrant sitting in the clouds awaiting every opportunity to foil personal goals and dreams. He actually cares about what is going on down here. In fact, Jesus described God using two simple, yet profound words in Matthew 6 that shed light on what God is really like. As Jesus taught His disciples how to pray, He said, "This is how you should pray: '*Our Father* in heaven, hallowed be your name'" (Matt. 6:9, emphasis added).

God wants us to grow in our relationship in such a way as to think of Him as a Father. He wants us to allow the root system of our faith to dig deep enough in our understanding and appreciation that we move to the third level of relationship, Loving Father. Do you realize that in the Old Testament God was only called Father seven times? In Matthew 6 alone, Jesus calls Him Father ten times, and there are over seventy references to the paternal nature of God in the New Testament. God wants us to view Him as a Father, not as some mystical influence in the universe. We like that thought because we can know a person and have a relationship with a person.

Yet even to mention the title of father evokes negative emotions for many people because of bad experiences or childhood memories. Sometimes the word *father* brings to the surface fear, resentment, and even guilt. For instance, as a child you may have heard, "You just wait until your father gets home." Then you went to church, attended a Sunday School class, and heard, "We are to look at God as our Father." Very subtly, mixed emotions may have developed. Perhaps because of those mixed emotions which we would wrestle with two thousand years later, Jesus qualified our understanding by saying, "Our Father *in heaven*."

This reference has little to do with location, but more to do with a state of perfection. There is not an earthly father alive who is not somewhat aware of his own inadequacies and insecurities. But God as our Father is perfect. What does that mean? What kind of Father is our God in heaven?

OUR FATHER IN HEAVEN

First, God is a *passionate* Father. The psalmist reminds us: "As a father has compassion on his children, so the LORD has compassion on those who fear him" (Ps. 103:13). God is filled with compassion and wants us to realize we are loved and cared for. This is one of God's most outstanding and obvious characteristics. One day the disciples found themselves on the Sea of Galilee, and a storm was brewing. Anyone who has ever been on the Sea of Galilee even today can attest to how quickly a storm can develop. The boat containing these disciples started to take in water because of the turbulence. With the boat beginning to sink, these terrified disciples asked the ultimate question, "Lord, don't you care?"

Have you ever felt like that? "Lord, where are You when I really need You?" "God, I'm going under. Don't You care?" But the careful student of the Bible will remember the promise found in 1 Peter 5:7, "Cast all your anxiety on him because he cares for you." Does God care about your health? Yes! Does He care about the checkbook that never seems to balance? Yes! What about that relationship that has never become what you hoped it would? Yes, He does care!

Too often in our spiritual life—although we may need to love God more—there is a much higher need to recognize just how much He loves us. When our relationship is such that we feel God's love and His passion for His children, we naturally begin to love Him more.

Second, God is a *persistent* Father. In other words, you can always count on Him because He's worthy of our trust and He never changes. James tells us, "Every good and perfect gift is from above, coming down from the Father of the heavenly lights, who does not change like shifting shadows" (James 1:17). Earthly fathers can be so unpredictable, as can any human being. Some teenagers will tell you, "I just don't know what to expect from my dad. One minute he's silent; the next he's violent. One minute he lets me have my way; the next he's unpredictable. I just can't figure him out." The result of this kind of inconsistency is insecurity.

But think for a moment about the persistent nature of our heavenly Father. He does not have good days and bad days. He never gets out of bed on the wrong side. (Maybe that's because He never goes to bed!)[1] And because of His grace, He loves us persistently on our good days and on our bad days. His nature is revealed to us in 2 Timothy 2:13, "If we are faithless, he will remain faithful, for he cannot disown himself." Is that not incredible? Even when I struggle, even when I am faithless and filled with doubt, God is persistent as my Father. Despite the fact that everything else around me may be changing, and my world appears to be falling apart, there is always one thing I can count on. God never changes how He acts toward me no matter what I do.

Glen recalls the precious times he and his wife Nancy have spent putting their three children to bed. On one occasion, he was putting his youngest son David to bed and asked him, "When does Daddy love you the most, when you're fighting with your brother or when you're a good boy?" David's answer? "Both times." Not anticipating this answer, Glen probed further, "Why, Son?" And little nine-year-old David said, "Cause I'm your Boomer." The nickname "Boomer" has always been a special name for David in the Martin family, and David knows that, no matter what, he will always be Glen's "Boomer."

God the Father loves us in a similar way. He loves us unconditionally and persistently because we are His boomers, His children. So when God shares a promise—and there are over four thousand promises in the Bible—you can count on them. Too many children face periods of rebellion and resentment in the home primarily because of broken promises by the parents. Why were they broken? Not enough ability. Not enough time. Not enough money. Not enough education. *The Living Bible* paraphrases Psalm 18:30a as "What a God he is! How perfect in every way! All his promises prove true." If God said it, you can count on it. He is consistent.

Third, God is a *personal* Father. He always has time for each one of His children, individually. He will always be there when we need Him. The apostle Paul was in the city of Athens one day having a heart-to-heart talk with the intellectuals of his day. He told them that God does not live in man-made buildings: "God did this so that men would seek him and perhaps reach out for him and find him, though he is not far from each one of us" (Acts 17:27). God is both millions of miles away and right next to you as you read these words. Sadly, we seldom see this approach to parenting today. So many homes struggle because of absentee parents, caught in the rat race of life, trying to maintain a level of living which hinders closeness and intimacy at home.

Your heavenly Father is the exact opposite. He is never too busy for you. Psalm 145:18 tells us, "The LORD is near to all who call on him, to all who call on him in truth." Do you know what this means? It means when you pray, you will never get a busy signal. He is never more concerned about a crisis in Europe than He is with your individual problem. In fact, never forget that God loves to meet your needs. Matthew 7:11 says, "If you, then, though you are evil, know how to give good gifts to your children, how much more will your Father in heaven give good gifts to those who ask him!" Earthly parents enjoy giving gifts to their children, and they are imperfect. Just imagine how much more a perfect Father knows how to take care of His children. Jesus said, "So do not worry saying, 'What shall we eat?' or 'What shall we drink?' or "What shall we wear?' For the pagans run after these things, and your heavenly Father knows that you need them" (Mat. 6:31–32). And remember, your heavenly Father has unlimited resources. He is not limited by time, space, or energy.

What a wonderful thing to realize how much God is sympathetic to our hurts. Are you feeling down today? God understands. And despite our regular habit of hiding our pain, you cannot hide it from God. Psalm 34:18 states, "The LORD is close to the brokenhearted and saves those who are crushed in spirit." Had a tough week, a tough year, even a tough life? God is near. Talk to Him about it. He cares and can help.

Jesus had a very special term He used to describe the personal nature of God. He called Him, "Abba." *Abba* is an Aramaic word used to describe the most intimate, personal nature of a father. We might use the word *Daddy.* This is the type of closeness God wants us to enjoy, because He is a personal Father.

Fourth, God is a *prepared* Father. Nothing surprises our Heavenly Father because He is capable of handling every situation. We are told in Luke 1:37: "For nothing is impossible with God." What great news. We may have limitations, but not our Father in heaven. In fact, do you realize the extent to which He desires to meet your needs? Ephesians 3:20 tells us, "Now to him who is able to do immeasurably more than all we ask or imagine, according to his power that is at work within us. . . ."

We wish we could list for you the many limitations of earthly fathers. And amazingly their earthly children often think they can fix anything, from decapitated G.I. Joe men to the flat tire on their bike. "Give it to Dad. He can fix anything." But as we grow older, we soon learn that even Dad has limitations. When it comes to allowances, Dad had limited resources. When it comes to advice, sometimes he is just guessing too. And at times he is just plain wrong.

Human fathers have limitations, but our heavenly Father has unlimited knowledge, resources, and power. Therefore, we need to stop looking everywhere else to get our needs met. We cannot look to our spouse or our boyfriend or girlfriend or even our boss; we can only look to God. We must remember He is a completely capable Father who always takes care of His children.

Fifth, God is a *permanent* Father. Approximately four thousand years ago our loving God guided His children out of Egypt. They came to the Red Sea, God parted the waters, and the people of Israel rejoiced with God's faithfulness to them. Three days later, they were found complaining and questioning that which God had displayed to them just a few miles back.

Two thousand years later, a band of twelve hand-chosen disciples saw the power of God displayed through the Lord Jesus, as He performed the incredible miracle of feeding the five thousand. As we have already noted, a similar opportunity soon came their way to exercise faith in feeding four thousand others, but they too questioned the permanence of Jesus' ability.

We see this same attitude in our day and age. If you were to be honest, you might be able to remember a time when you responded in the same manner. You may have seen God's handiwork in your life, yet you later questioned if God could work in those ways ever again. Ask yourself these questions: Has God changed? Is He no longer the caring Father you need Him to be?

Charles Stanley's son, Andy, is a youth pastor. In trying to teach teenagers what it means to have faith and trust in God, he came up with a wonderful object lesson. One year just before camp he went to the bank, got $315 in small bills, and headed off to the camp. On the last day, after stuffing the money in his pockets, he asked for the person with the most money left to come up on stage. A young man responded with $226 in his wallet. Asked if he trusted Andy, the youth loudly proclaimed he definitely did. Then Andy asked, "I want you to give me all your money. I will not give it back, but I will give you what is in my pockets, and I can assure you it is well worthwhile." The young man blanched and then declined. "But don't you trust me? Aren't I worthy of your trust?" Andy asked. "Yes, but . . . ." and the deal was never completed. When Andy pulled out the bills and slowly counted them—and they ended up $99 more than the young man had—the object lesson was driven home to the heart of each teenager.

Action Step LF-5

Probe the depth of a loving, heavenly Father by answering these questions. Can you trust someone who wants the very best for you and has the ability to supply it for you? How would a perfect, loving, heavenly Father respond to you when you have done something wrong? How would He respond when you ask Him for something that is good? What about something that is not good for you?

ENTER THE ENEMY

Our Loving Father will never leave you; that is His promise to us. But the enemy of our souls wants us to doubt God and to question His ability. You would think we would learn. But not too long ago Lenin said if you told a big enough lie long enough, people would believe it. Ever wonder where he learned that truth? From the father of lies undoubtedly! Satan has used this trick from the very beginning of human history.

In the Garden of Eden our first parents were set up to live happily ever after, having been placed in a paradise-like setting by a loving, personal God. They had been given everything they could ever want—virtually carte blanche to the earth and all it had, with only one *small* restriction: "Don't eat of the tree of the knowledge of good and evil." What a simple, innocuous request. How easy to obey—or so we say today.

But when they were enticed by the Tempter, they fell into his trap of questioning the love and goodness of the One from whom they had only experienced good. What a monstrous, lie.

But they bought it hook, line, and sinker! And mankind has been wretched ever since, apart from God's intervention!

We do the same today. We willingly swallow the lie that we cannot trust our heavenly Father. We allow our earthly hurts from parents or others in authority to distort our view and our understanding of God. For many feelings, emotions, fears, and human experiences effectively block a clear perception of God, stifling all truth about Him.

So what do we do if we have a damaged view of God because of our parents or some other authority figure? First, we have to recognize and identify that there is a problem. For most it is extremely obvious, for they daily are affected by their past no matter how old they may be. Many people feel crippled emotionally because a parent was not loving in their actions.

Dian remembers talking with a friend, Carey, whose mother always used to yell at her whenever she displeased her mom. Too often a hand struck out, a foot kicked, a tongue wounded, and often a loud and angry voice accompanied. As an adult, Carey was emotionally unable to have anyone disagree with her or correct her. It affected her relationship with her husband, as well as with those at work. She almost always felt threatened, fearful, and intimidated by any voice that was above a normal conversational level. She would immediately retreat and hide emotionally from the person, even though no one else would see the individual as being a threat. This problem came close to destroying her marriage, for her husband would often use a strong voice to emphasize a point, even when he was not unhappy. Frequent misunderstandings and tension plagued their relationship. The experiences of her childhood were used by the enemy to damage her marriage and her relationship with God.

She wanted desperately to trust God, but even though she loved Him, she could not commit completely to Him because of her own fears of being controlled. She often felt inadequate and unworthy of God's love. She also found herself not wanting to displease Him so He would not "yell" at her or show any disapproval. This caused her to stop serving Him, so she would not be vulnerable to criticism for falling short of any expectations He may have had of her. It was not until she dealt with her feelings toward her mother that she was able to resolve her problems both with individuals and with God.

Carey's situation was minor compared to Flo's. As a child Flo had been physically and emotionally abused and violated by several relatives. Her emotions were so repressed that she had blocked much of the hurt out and at first only acknowledged two key authority figures physically violating her. She was unaware her birth father had started the whole sordid cycle that had led her finally into casual prostitution.

Once saved she still had problems, and many of those lay not only with her husband, but also with her view of God. In her eyes He was good, but definitely not Someone to be trusted. Had she not trusted three men in her own life who were supposed to protect her, but who in fact had violated her? What they did, He probably would do, so she could not risk committing herself to Him. She had been hurt so much in the past that she needed to protect herself from any other possible source of pain—God included.

We could give you numerous other scenarios, all based on this theme of an authority figure not being perfect. Whatever may be the source of a person's reservations about God as a Father, it is important to deal with the twisted piece of the puzzle from the enemy and to replace it with the correct piece—a right perception of God as good, kind, loving, gentle, patient, and, in fact, perfect.

So what do you do when you have a distorted father image? In fact, you may be wondering if this is part of your own problem. These questions may help you identify if you are allowing a negative human relationship to interfere with having a close relationship with your Loving Father.

As you read the following questions, check each one that you would answer "yes":

☐ Do you find it easier to relate to Jesus than to the Father?

☐ Do you inwardly bristle when told to do something?

☐ Are you afraid of being asked by God to do something you may not want to do?

☐ Is it hard to trust God with *every* detail of your life?

☐ Are you afraid you may have to give up something if you serve God or tell Him He can have His way in your life?

☐ Do you sometimes feel God is sitting up in heaven, just waiting for you to make a mistake?

☐ Are there things you wouldn't want God to ask you to do because you just don't want to do them?

☐ Do you feel God is disappointed in you, or not pleased with you?

☐ Do you feel God wants you to do or not to do certain things in order to get His goals accomplished—despite how you feel?

☐ Is God sometimes unreasonable in what He expects of you?

☐ Is there one or more verses in the Bible you avoid reading because you know you don't live up to what is asked, and at this point in your life you are not willing to deal with it?

☐ Do you see God as someone who is too busy running the universe to bother with your small problems?

☐ Are you afraid to ask God for certain things because you are sure He will say no?

☐ Do you feel uncertain of your relationship with the Father—that He may not be pleased with you or that you may do something that will disqualify you from heaven?

If you answered yes to any of the above questions, you probably need to work on your view of authority, especially as it relates to God. The old sin nature can cause some of the problems, but more than likely these areas of weakness in trusting God completely are created by someone in a position of authority over you—usually a father, but sometimes a mother. And they need to be forgiven.

In what we call the Lord's Prayer, Jesus set up an element for forgiveness some of us need to consider seriously: "Forgive us our debts, as we also have forgiven our debtors" (Matt. 6:12). I am to be forgiven in the same way I have forgiven someone else. Jesus did not leave us wondering what He meant. He says two verses later, "For if you forgive men when they sin against you, your heavenly Father will also forgive you. But if you do not forgive men their sins, your Father will not forgive your sins" (vv. 14–15). There are no qualifications here as to what degree of hurt I experienced, but rather it is unlimited in scope. In other words, if I am to receive forgiveness, it will be the same kind I give to all who need forgiveness from me. If I refuse to forgive someone, then I will be unforgiven. Thus, forgiveness becomes even more important than it seemed to be at first glance. Jesus takes it out of the "Optional" column and places it squarely in the "Must Do" column.[2]

But we are convinced this is not because He wants to be unreasonable. He wants us to realize how devastating and how destructive unforgiveness is. Because of God's great love for us, He wants our best, as would any good father. Today medical science shows us what God knew all along: Unforgiveness causes all kinds of problems both mental and physical. There is no time to cover it all here, but suffice it to say the one who consciously or unconsciously refuses to forgive suffers definite consequences for it. Thus, God strongly emphasizes the need to do so.

If you are struggling with unforgiveness, we suggest you go through the following action step.

Action Step LF-6

It is important to remove any barriers between you and the Lord if you are to draw closer to Him and grow in your faith. Otherwise these barriers block your roots of faith from going deeper into the Lord. Therefore, if you answered yes to any of the questions on page 94, then consider the following points:

- Write what you feel about the source(s) of your hurt, your hesitation.

- Identify your current feelings: There is no forgiveness; The person does not deserve forgiving; You tried to forgive, but could not. Determine you are going to forgive.

Remember, forgiveness starts in the head, and then the heart responds at some time in the future. We forgive in obedience to the command of the Lord.[3] If you still are having troubles, some good books that address this problem are written by Neil Anderson. They have proven to be very helpful for many who have past hurts and distorted images of God.[4]

- Ask God to help you forgive. You may want to pray along these lines:

Loving, Heavenly Father,
I have been hurt by _____. *It is hard to forgive him/her but I know You want me to do so. Therefore, I am choosing, as an act of my will, to forgive* _____
for (name the actions) *and for the hurt and damage it has done to me emotionally and physically. I choose to forgive* _____ *for the way this is currently interfering in my life by* (name any specific things you are aware of that are being influenced negatively by this person's treatment of you, no matter how long ago it has been). *Lord, help the hurts from* _____ *to no longer interfere in my feelings toward You. I want to trust You fully and to have no barriers between us.*

An additional prayer you might use in this area of repairing your relationship with the Father is:

Father,
I have been hurt by _____ *in the past. This hurt is causing me to feel (the lie of Satan) toward You. Yet in my*

*head and from the Scriptures I know You are (the truth).
Help me to trust You and bring my feelings into line with
the truth. Please show me any time I start to believe a lie.*

- When negative thoughts come back, thank God you have forgiven the person, even if you do not have such feelings yet. Pray positive things for the person such as God's blessing, leading, meeting of needs, and that they will find satisfaction through the Lord in whatever they do. Do not use your prayer like a weapon. Instead, use it to pray good things for the person even if you do not feel they deserve it.

STEPS TO FORGIVENESS AND RECOVERY

Forgiving parents is critically important for unforgiveness can interfere with the process of drawing closer. Sometimes we have trouble loving God and drawing closer to Him because our understanding is somewhat childlike. It is rooted in an incorrect perception due to our upbringing at home.

Dennis Guernsey writes: "Many parents communicate a sense of security and well-being to their children which allows those children to grow into mature, healthy adults able to return God's love. Unfortunately, not all parent-child relationships have this result. Parents can communicate negative messages which indirectly hinder their children from having a healthy relationship with God."[5] He develops the idea that some parents perceive the world as overwhelming and depressing. Others view the world as entirely evil. Both of these convictions lead to anxiety and fear because the parents may have spent their energy protecting their child, not preparing them.

If you are having trouble drawing closer because of past parental struggles, here are four simple steps to recovery.

First, face the facts. When Jesus said that the truth will set you free, we believe there was a two-fold implication. Of course, a transformation takes place as the result of the gospel. We have covered this in depth in chapter 4 on the Sacrificial Savior. But there is also the matter of embracing the truth about life and its problems, realizing that God is at work in any and every situation. To know that all that happens to me is drawing me closer to God is quite freeing.

Second, forgive the parent. Once you have faced the fact that you did have problems as a child and have indeed been hurt, forgiveness must be the next step. Our parents were not perfect, and thus they have failed us. When the hurt is allowed to fester, resentment is the natural consequence which will affect your relationship with God. This is why forgiveness is important.

Third, focus the healing. Many carry around the world on their shoulders in the form of guilt. God never intended for you to be the general manager of the universe; He wants you to be freed from this bondage. By focusing on Jesus Christ's healing touch and tenderness, not on the pain you have experienced, the weight will become bearable. As 1 Peter 5:7 states: "Cast all your anxiety on him for he cares for you."

Some memories may seem overwhelming; you may wonder if the pain will ever leave. These types of hurts may need professional assistance to handle. This does not indicate a flaw in your personality or a sign of weakness however; in fact, seeking help indicates strength.

Fourth, find the community. The church is not only a community of redemption, but also one of caring. Relationships and friendships need to develop to restore inner healing from the damage of your youth and to maintain a healthy, balanced outlook. Find a church, a community of Christians to grow with, lean on, and care for. Jesus knew we would need a body of believers to grow in our faith. Never underestimate the power of fellowship.

Seeking a Deeper Walk with the Father

Many people in their search for a deepening walk with God resemble a soldier on sentry duty. Suddenly he hears footsteps approaching in the dark. His first words are, "Who goes there?" In the middle of our personal times of crisis and struggle, we, too, want to know who is out there.

The answer to all three cries of desperation is God the Father. And He awaits our desire to draw close to Him as His children. But how? In a world with so much confusion, what steps can we take to draw closer to Him?

Action Step LF-7

Commit to deepen your prayer life. There is something unique about a parent's ability to know the needs of their children before they ask. God the Father is no exception. When we ask God to help us get closer to Him, we are not asking for something new. Long before the words were uttered, God knew our heart. The fact that God's eye never misses one detail of our life can bring us great comfort. Your Father knows what you need before you ask Him. And let us add that your heavenly Father even knows what you need when it is *contrary* to what you ask. You can talk all you want about whatever you want in your prayers, chatter like a three-year-old, argue like a prosecuting attorney, but not for one second will God be diverted from giving His attention to the primary need in your life—despite the fact that you do not want to talk about it.

To deepen your prayer life is to recognize that God knows your deepest secrets and desires. And it means that you are ready to see your Father as any parent who looks upon his child when they are hurting. The little child may not be able to verbalize what is wrong, but Daddy knows. And thank God that our prayers are not dependent upon our ability to express correctly what is on our heart. It does not depend upon our making the correct diagnosis of our situation and then presenting them to God in some organized, properly phrased prayer deposition.

Think for a moment about the paralytic in Mark 2. He was carried past the crowd, up onto the rooftop. The roof was torn away and he was lowered into the presence of Jesus. Can you imagine what he would have been feeling, gazing into the penetrating eyes of Jesus? Can you see his beseeching look, asking Him to save him? "Make me well, Lord. I do not know quite how to ask, but please, please do something to heal me."

He did not have to say a word. Jesus heard his unspoken prayer quite differently from the way his friends had intended. Jesus told the man, "Your sins are forgiven" (v. 5). The paralytic's real pain lay in the fact that he was separated from God; this needed divine attention first. Then, after forgiveness had taken place, Jesus could take away his illness. Jesus knew what the sick man needed before he asked—and knew it would be contrary to his first request.

A deepening prayer life recognizes why so many prayers seem to go unanswered, although they are answered in a way that is totally different from what we may have asked for. A deepening prayer life understands that "Father knows best," and this will sometimes be opposite to what we may envision and pursue.

It is no wonder why the words preceding the Lord's Prayer describe this attribute of God by saying, "And when you are praying, do not use meaningless repetition, as the Gentiles do, for they suppose that they will be heard for their many words. Therefore do not be like them; *for your Father knows what you need, before you ask Him*" (Matt. 6:7–8, NASB, emphasis added).

Two ideas leap out of those final words in this passage. *First, God is always there before I pray.* The purpose of our praying and asking is not to present our case carefully in defense of a position, nor to remind God in case He forgets, but to seek Him as our Father. We are His children. We are the Lord's brothers *and sisters*. Therefore, He already knows everything and can still make something out of our trivial, sometimes meaningless, prayers.

Second, when God does not seem to answer our prayers, this is not because He is indifferent to us or hard of hearing. He knows our cries as only a Father can know, but sometimes He prescribes healing remedies for our ailments, more bitter than the ones we would chose.

The key to praying and drawing closer to God is to enter into communion or a deeper fellowship with the Father and to get to know Him better. Thus we study the attributes. If you can honestly say nothing more than "Dear Heavenly Father," the main objective has already happened.

GOD'S NAMES REVEAL HIS NATURE

What's in a name? In our time and present society, we do not spend as much time naming our children as people in the past. But most of us have at least attempted to look up the meaning of our name just for fun. Many parents, when naming their children, use titles that sound nice or that may honor a relative and that do not associate with some past memory which creates ill-feelings and pain.

But despite our culture's lack of emphasis on choosing a name, in the time of Abraham, David, and the prophets of old, names were common nouns and verbs and thus filled with color and meaning. The Hebrews attached great significance to God's name, which you find throughout the Psalms. In those days names really meant something special, for they represented your character. The names for God that we find in our Bibles represent all that He is, His attributes. And hear this well: No single name can describe all of God's attributes. No single name can describe all that God is. So we need to examine what God's names tell us about Him.

Realizing that there are many names for God in our Bibles, look at how studying three names of God can expand your understanding of God and impact your faith and life.

One classic example in the Old Testament is in the life of Abraham when he was told to offer his only son, Isaac, as an offering. He went up to Mt. Moriah and built an altar in preparation for what God had asked him to do. Just as he had raised his knife to sacrifice his son in obedience to God, however, an angel appeared and said, "Stop. I'll supply the sacrifice." And there Abraham looked over and saw a ram in the thicket that was going to be the burnt offering. Abraham named that place "The LORD will provide" (Gen. 22:14a). The Hebrew wording is *Yahweh-Jireh*, "God is my provider." In our times of water shortages, power shortages, financial shortages, and time shortages, what great news it is to know that God is Jehovah-Jireh, a God who provides and never runs out of resources.

In Jeremiah 23:6b we read, "This is the name by which he will be called: The LORD Our Righteousness." *Yahweh-Tsidkenu* is the Hebrew which means "God is our righteousness." God likes to make wrong things right. Do you have anything wrong in your life that you would like to have made right? God wants to do it. Actually most people run around today under a load of guilt. They carry regrets about the past and missed opportunities. But God has good news when you feel guilty: "I, even I, am he who blots out your transgressions, for my own sake, and remembers your sins no more" (Isa. 43:25). Why does God forgive? Because you earn it? No, because He is *Yahweh-Tsidkenu*, our Righteousness.

Judges 6:24 records another name for God. We are told, "So Gideon built an altar to the LORD there and called it 'The LORD is Peace.'" Here was Gideon, appointed by God as the sixth judge over Israel at a time of sin, oppression, and paganism. Afraid for his life, stressed out by his circumstances, he began to worship God, and found a sense of peace than can never be found anywhere else. "The Lord is Peace," is the translation of the Hebrew, *Yahweh-Shalom*.

The problem with our world is that we are over-committed, uptight, and stressed out. People will go to great lengths in order to find peace. They try therapies, fads, seminars, tapes, long vacations, alcohol, and drugs. People cry for a sense of peace but cannot find it. Whenever they identify a shortage, they are equally willing to provide a synthetic means of replacing it. And God says, "No, I want to give you real peace in a relationship with *Yahweh-Shalom.*"

Every need you have in life is covered by the attributes revealed in one of the names of God. Although we do not have time to cover them all, you need to quit looking to other people and other places and other circumstances to have those needs met. This is why there is a list of the major names of God in resource 5. The more you get to know God as Father, the more you will see that you do not have to worry or feel guilty or be afraid or have to hurt anymore.

Action Step LF-8

Using resource 5, add each name of God to the appropriate attribute page in your journal. For example, "Jehovah Shalom" would go on the page marked at the top "Peace." If you do not yet have a page for any particular name of God, then make a new one for this attribute/name.

At this point you will find some things that will enable you to avoid enemy pitfalls and hindrances in your walk with the Lord.

You need to recognize an Enemy Attack. You may have some of the following fear-filled, intimidating thoughts:

- "Your own father was not trustworthy, so don't trust God."

- "This material is too painful to go through. You really don't need this extra pain it will cause." (This lie is one designed to keep you in bondage so you will not experience freedom. If you do not lance a wound, the infection stays and things get worse.)

- "God will ask something very undesirable of you if you yield to His will."

- "If you go further in these levels, you are going to have to give up too much. It won't be worth the sacrifice."

Action Step LF-9

Update the response chart you started in action step SS-6.

Action Step LF-10

Determine what you can do to please God. Undoubtedly God has been showing you what He wants you to yield to Him or improve in. Allow the Holy Spirit to give you His power and ability to do these things. For example, does He want you to be more loving, in control of anger, less afraid, more trusting, kinder, more patient. Look at Galatians 5:22–23 which lists the fruits of the Spirit, along with 1 Corinthians 13 on love. Are there some things here you should ask for?

Action Step LF-11

Review regularly and add to your list of benefits. Are you having greater peace, confidence, and security, or a brighter future? Continue to thank God for what He has done and for your developing relationship.

Action Step LF-12

As you grow closer to the Lord, you should find your own self-image improving. You might want to keep a running commentary that you update periodically to tell yourself what you think about you and what you think God thinks about you. If these comments are less than positive, you will most likely be looking at a lie of the enemy. You will need to present that to the Lord for His removal and pray and seek His perspective.

Once as Glen took a very crowded flight home, a family was separated from one another due to seating arrangements. The two-year-old son was given to the mother to take care of and the dad went to the rear of the plane to find his seat. All went well until the plane had taken off. Then the two-year-old decided he wanted to be with his father. Mom did everything she could to console her son. Glen watched her play cards, draw pictures, and read magazines—each for about three minutes. But this child wanted his daddy. Mom restrained him as long as she could but nothing was going to squelch this kid's desire to be with his father. When all was safe, Mom gladly let him go.

Hearing a story like this may remind you of Psalm 42:1–2 which reminds us, "As the deer pants for streams of water, so my soul pants for you, O God. My soul thirsts for God, for the living God. When can I go and meet with God?"

Developing a strong root system down to the level of Loving Father will generate the same kinds of feelings and desires spoken about by the psalmist and practiced by the little boy in the airplane. Spending time with your loving, heavenly Father is not something you have to do, but something you cannot wait to do. But as good as this level is, the next is even better. You need to check the questions in chapter 2 to see if you now qualify for that level. When you do, begin your walk with your Faithful Companion. He is waiting to take your hand.

◆

1. Psalm 121:3–4.

2. See Jesus' very strong teaching in Matthew 6:14–15.

3. We deal in some detail with forgiveness in our book *Power House*. In the resources of that book is a section on how to pray for a difficult person in your life.

4. Neil Anderson, *Victory Over Darkness* and *The Bondage Breaker* (Harvest House,1990).

5. Dennis Guernsey, *Sometimes It's Hard to Love God (Downers Grove, Ill.: InterVarsity Press, 1989),* 30.

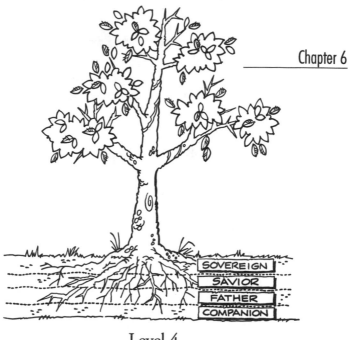

Chapter 6

Level 4
Faithful Companion

And what does the LORD require of You? To act justly
and to love mercy and to walk humbly with your God.

MICAH 6:8

Action Step FC-1

Read Philippians. This book was written by Paul, whom God
chose to minister to the Gentiles (non-Jews). List the things you
read about God and His will for your life, and about how to live
successfully with others. While listing these principles, you may
want to think about how they apply to your life or how you
would like them to apply. If appropriate, list specific principles
you have seen in your own experiences with the Lord. You may
also want to ask God to do that specific thing in your life or to
increase a positive quality that is already there. Note any verses
you will want to memorize now or later, such as Philippians
4:13, 19. These are great verses for increasing your faith.

There is a wonderful story of a young man who sought out a wise, old philosopher. The young man wanted to learn from the sage, so when he found the old man sitting by a lake, he asked, "Sir, I would like to sit at your feet, be your disciple, and learn wisdom from you."

The sage did not reply. Instead he stood up, approached the young man, and shoved him into the water. Then he jumped in on top of the boy and held his head under water. Taking in water, the lad was surprised and confused. Thoughts swirled in his head. *This must be a joke! He will let me up in a minute.*

But as the air escaped in bubbles to the surface and his lungs screamed for oxygen, he suddenly realized this was not a joke! He would soon drown if he did not resist. Arms flaying, he was able to throw the old man off and surface for a gulp of air. But suddenly he was pushed down again. Fear and anger swept over him, and he once again was able to throw off the old man.

Screaming, the young man exploded, "You are crazy! I came to learn from you, wanting to be your disciple, and you try to kill me!" Then the sage replied in a soft, but firm voice, "Young man, when you want to learn from me as much as you wanted to get out of the water, only then will you be ready to learn."

Deuteronomy 4:29 states, "If . . . you seek the LORD your God, you will find him if you look for him with all your heart and with all your soul." God tells us in Micah 6:8 the manner in which we are to walk with Him: "He has showed you, O man, what is good. And what does the LORD require of you? To act justly and to love mercy and to walk humbly with your God." God is ready to teach us, to let us be with Him, to be a true and faithful companion—if we will seek such a relationship.

PROFILE OF A COMPANION

Companions come in all sizes and shapes and for various reasons. A dog can be your companion, an elderly person can hire a companion to accompany them, or at times airlines offer to let you buy one ticket and get a free one for a companion.

You can even pick up a hitchhiker and have him be your companion for a long or a short stretch of driving. But we will examine a very specific kind of companion: the teacher-mentor.

How would you describe a relationship as a companion to someone, and how would this relate to being a companion to God? Four areas seem to be obvious ingredients. God defines the first one: "Do two walk together unless they have agreed to do so?" (Amos 3:3). So *agreement* is the first requirement. You have to want to spend time together. With God we know this is the desire of His heart. He tells us in many different ways in the Word that He desires to be with us.

Second, you would *share experiences* together because you are together by definition. One of the special privileges we have as believers is sharing our heart with God and in turn learning more about His heart toward us and others. We get to see His overwhelming goodness, infinite patience, unchanging love, and unending mercies as we read the Bible—His love letter and "owner's manual" to us. The Holy Spirit makes the Word come alive to our hearts and points things out from it that are specifically for us and our situation.

Third, there should be *conversation*. Not just one way, but rather an exchange of ideas from both parties. Think of your own experience. When you have been with someone who monopolizes the conversation, or who does not let you talk but only wants you to listen, you feel uneasy, dominated, and useless in the conversation. You may feel you are only a listening board, and your opinion matters little since it is rarely sought.

Sometimes we are guilty of doing this to God: We rush into His presence with our "want" list and then, in essence, after presenting our requests and/or complaints, we close the time with "In Jesus' name, Amen." No time to hear His input, no time to seek His advice. Only a time for us to "dump" on Him. Peter advised us in 1 Peter 5:7 to give the Lord all our burdens and cares. Yes, we *are* to present our anxieties to Him, but then we are supposed to wait for His response.

Unfortunately, many people seem stuck at the Loving Father level and never really seek Him with all their hearts. They are content to learn as a child would—that is, learning and following rules in order to avoid big problems—but not as willing to spend any great period of time with the Lord in the free time they have. There is little delight in the relationship, only obedience out of necessity. They have what we used to call "fire insurance" Christianity. They have salvation from the penalty of sin, but they will enter heaven "through the flames" (1 Cor. 3:15). They have yet to cross that line of spiritual familial relationship into spiritual heart relationship.

What do we mean by spiritual heart relationship? Let's look at a human illustration to see the difference. Some children grow up in families where their father is a strong disciplinarian. They obey because they do not want to suffer the wrath of their father. Although they may even respect the father and his accomplishments, they want nothing to do with him on a personal basis. It is not unusual for such children to dread the return of their dad in the evening. As adults they spend as little time with him as possible. There is the physical relationship with obedience, but not the close heart relationship. Fear and mistrust are barriers to their ever being close.

On the other hand, some have fathers who have definite standards and rules to obey, but the relationship is one of love and respect. They are excited when Dad walks through the door at night. They love the weekends because Dad can be with them and they do fun things together. Such children obey because they love and trust their father, not because they fear him or the consequences of disobedience. Thus, in our relationship to God we can respond and obey either out of love or out of fear.

When one is in a healthy relationship with God, there is a fourth element, *learning*. As we spend time with Him, our relationship allows us to learn about Him, about ourselves, and about others. We come to appreciate Him more as we get to know Him better. We become more relaxed in His presence as we now are His companion.

We understand ourselves better—our strengths and weaknesses, how to overcome them, why we do things the way we do, how to change our negative responses, and the like. We also learn much about others and how better to interact with them, showing forth all the fruit of the Spirit.

TRACING OUR JOURNEY TILL NOW

At this fourth level you are probably experiencing a change. In order better to identify this change, let's take a moment to look at how we got here.

In our journey to know God, we went through the Holy Sovereign stage where He was at arms length and had no real relationship with us apart from being our Creator and Sovereign. We saw Him with all His *awesome qualities*—all-powerful, all-knowing, eternal, and the like.

From there we beheld Him as our Sacrificial Savior and we saw some of the more *personal qualities* of His being good and caring for us, loving and forgiving us. We responded by acknowledging His authority in our life and submitting to Him. In so doing we formed a new relationship as we invited Jesus into our lives. Getting to know the pertinent attributes of God at this second level was for many a new experience, with many facets of His nature still hidden.

However, as we moved into knowing Him as our Loving Father and seeing even more of His gentle heart toward us, we may have come to a barrier He needed to help us overcome. It is at this level we had to allow Him to reshape our understanding of what a "Father" is and to undo any misconceptions earthly fathers or authority figures may have created that warped our perception of God as our Loving Father.

Even at this level, we usually learn new, aspects of His nature. We will never discover all there is to know about Him, but by the time we reach the level of Faithful Companion, we start to get a better grasp of who God truly is and the nature of His relationship with us. Faith and trust are increasing, and we commit ourselves at a deeper level.

Dian has a good friend, Nancy. They met a few years ago because Nancy wanted to learn certain prayer skills from Dian. Nancy came to her to be mentored, this meant spending time together both in ministry and personally. Their relationship has grown beyond mentoring into a deep friendship. In fact, because of her teaching and writing skills, Nancy was able to help with this book when the deadline was set up and time was at a premium. Both benefit from the relationship because friendship developed out of the companion-mentoring stage.

This is not always the progression in our relationship with the Lord, but it can be. As Loving Father and Faithful Companion, He offers a strong degree of mentoring or teaching and modeling. As this happens, we start to take on His value system.

As part of the transition from Loving Father to Faithful Companion, we turn a corner in our relationship. We find Him less an authority figure and more a desirable companion Who is no less in charge in our lives. Our perception of the relationship is changing. We now realize He is on our side, how much He wants the best for us and how absolutely dependable He is. The inborn, unhealthy fear of God that stems from our sin nature, and is often stirred up by the enemy of our souls, is weakening as we are getting a clearer picture of who He really is.

GOD AS OUR FAITHFUL COMPANION

So here we are at the next level—that of Faithful Companion. Throughout our lives, we look for those rare individuals with whom we feel relaxed and comfortable and can share our heart and our secrets and know they will not betray us, who will always be there for us, and in whom we can have confidence—individuals we can respect and who in turn admire us and want us to be successful.

God wants to be in that type of a role with us, but He is even better than any earthly companion. For God is a perfect companion: the One who knows the road we are traveling on and all of the problems that lay ahead; the One who can give us dependable advice; the One who wants to share our life with us and will not put us down when we stumble; the One who will never desert us if we fail or do not live up to His standards. He accepts us just as we are, wants to be with us forever, is able to help us be all that we can be, and can enable us either to avoid or overcome every obstacle or problem in our life.

As our Companion, He is also our Loving Father, our Sacrificial Savior, and our Holy Sovereign. All of the attributes we have learned about Him up till now are still true about Him, but we find even greater depths and aspects of these attributes as we walk further with Him at this new level. We will discover new attributes or at least become more aware of new ones, and see different facets of the ones we already know as we share our journey together.

Action Step FC-2

As the second action step in this level, we want to examine more thoroughly ten new attributes. They are Kind, Compassionate, Wonderful, Encourager, Peace Giver, Counselor, Faithful, Empowerer, Giving, and Trustworthy. In resource 1 you will find an expanded study on each of these attributes of God which we recommend you read at this time.

Think about what these attributes mean to your own life, and ask yourself the following questions about them.

- If God were not kind, could I trust Him when He asks me to do something?

- If He were not compassionate, would I have confidence He understands my pain, my hurts, my fears?

- Even if He is compassionate, what if He were not all-powerful? Would I be able to have a strong trust in His compassion causing Him successfully to solve my specific problem? Maybe He wouldn't have this necessary power.

(This would especially be a strong factor in a case where there seems to be no solution and it is a seemingly impossible situation.)

- Where do I need His counsel? Where not?
- How important are faith and trust in God in my walk with Him?
- How secure would I feel in doing what He asks if I could not trust Him 100 percent?"

Christians who are drawing closer to God are doing so, in part, because trust in Him is growing. We are created by God with the ability to trust Him. But the enemy of our souls is constantly doing all He can to undermine this trust.

Action Step FC-3

Seek each day to better understand God's will. Turn to resource 6 for some good help in this area.

Aren't you glad that God provides seconds, third, and even tenth chances? This was a lesson Jonah soon learned. When Jonah was told to head in one direction, he chose the opposite, and God provided a little Mediterranean cruise to redirect him. In Jonah 3:1 we read, "Then the word of the LORD came to Jonah a second time." A fresh start. A new beginning.

But it is easy for us to forget this fact and Satan will do everything he can to take advantage of the situation. One of Satan's favorite lies is for us to believe that because we have experienced a past failure, we have probably missed out on God's perfect will for our lives. Can't you just hear Satan saying, "You've missed out on the best God had for you because of a wrong turn, bad decision. Oh, you'll get to heaven, but I will make you miserable until you get there."

Part of Satan's scheme is to convince God's children that God's will is a straight and narrow path between the two points of justification and sanctification. And God has provided you with just enough resources and power to make the journey *if* . . . you take the straight path, thus God's will. Let's illustrate this concept with the simple diagram below:

Justification   Sanctification

The problem with this kind of thinking is a failure to recognize that in God's timetable sometimes the shortest distance between two points is a zig-zag. So Christians become convinced that when they have taken a slight detour, God's limited resources and power run out and they will never "arrive." Look at the illustration below:

Justification   Sanctification

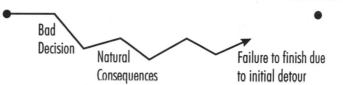

Granted, no one may ever live up entirely to God's ultimate plan and expectations for his or her life. But very few grasp the concept that the highest will of God is that now—wherever you find yourself, at whatever station of life—you do what pleases God the most and you will be in the center of God's will.

To live in the center of God's will and experience His companionship is the greatest thing that can happen to you. Romans 12:1–2 says, "Therefore, I urge you, brothers, in view of God's mercy, to offer your bodies as living sacrifices, holy and pleasing to God—which is your spiritual worship. Do not conform any longer to the pattern of this world, but be transformed by the renewing of your mind. Then you will be able to test and approve what God's will is—his good, pleasing and perfect will."

The psalmist shared the joy of living God's will in Psalm 23:1, "The LORD is my shepherd, I shall lack nothing." Even the Israelites in the Old Testament were told, "And now, O

Israel, what does the LORD your God ask of you but to fear the LORD your God, to walk in all his ways, to love him, to serve the LORD your God with all your heart and with all your soul" (Deut. 10:12). When you sense this reality in your life, you will move into a companionship you will enjoy for eternity.

Action Step FC-4

List any areas where you at this time do not fully trust God. Once you have identified these areas, use the suggested prayer or one of your own to ask God to strengthen this part of your faith and trust in Him. As always, be certain you pray this from your heart, and not just as words. If you find you cannot be sincere in such a prayer, go to resource 7 and pray the prayer of preparation. If you are still having troubles, then go to the Scriptures and read what the Lord has to say in the area of your hindrance. (A *Strong's* or *Young's Concordance* will help, or maybe a *Nave's Topical Bible*. Also, You may contact Dian for other materials at the address given in the "How to Use This Book" section.)

REMOVING A CRITICAL HINDRANCE

One of the hindrances to having God as our constant companion may lie in our desire to be independent. We may submit to Him as Father because we see no other choice. But to invite Him into a closer relationship, to have Him actually actively involved in *every area* of our lives—which happens when you have a constant companion—to have Him give His seal of approval to all we do—well, many find that too intimidating. Some people even find a closer relationship with people to be threatening. They like their space.

A few of us want to be independent and not have others—even God—tell or suggest what we should do. We can be certain if we have any of these tendencies (and even if we don't), that the adversary is going to use our weaknesses—our mistrust and self-centeredness—to try to keep us separated from God.

Action Step FC-5

If the Lord is showing you that this is a problem for you, pray something similar to the following. Make certain it expresses what you want to say to God.

> *Lord,*
> *I tend to be independent and want to do things on my own without others interfering—not even You. I know this is wrong, but I will need to give up a lifetime habit of being in control of my life. Help me, Holy Spirit, not only to want to do things Your way, but to have the courage to do whatever You show me to do. Help me submit every area of my life to You. Show me where I have not trusted in You fully and how to resist such doubts from now on. Give me Scripture to counter any enemy attack. Then help me to be happy in releasing all of this to You, in order to keep the enemy from making me feel bitter or resentful. Let me see it as a positive thing. I love You and trust You.*

Once hindrances are removed, you are ready to look at God as a Faithful Companion in more depth. Until now, obedience has been based on fear and gratitude/love. However, when we know God as our Companion, we will obey Him out of love more than out of selfish or fearful motives. Why? As we realize how good He truly is and how much He loves us, His Love will cause us to respond in love.[1] We will have worked through any problems we may have had in seeing Him as a Loving Father. When we are free to experience His love in a deeper way, we can obey Him from a heart that has been touched by this love. Our hearts will respond in a new and more open way because we will obey Him out of our love for Him, not out of necessity.

Such responses are easily seen in a marriage setting. The wife who obeys her husband only because she is afraid to incur his displeasure has a much different relationship with her spouse than does the wife who obeys because she loves her husband so much she would never do anything to disappoint or grieve him. It should be the same in our relationship with our God. Love is the key to obedience. It has been said that if people understood the love of God for them, pastors would never have to preach another sermon. Love is a powerful force; it transforms lives.

GOD FINE TUNES OUR LIVES

God will probably have begun to fine tune your life in order to strip away small hindrances. These things, even though so insignificant they may not bother others, are definite barriers to your developing companionship with the Lord.

Once you recognize any problem, you need to deal with it right away. Because you are nearing the final levels of intimacy with God, you should not have any hesitation to do so; however, the enemy of your soul will try to stop you from surrendering. But if you resist him, he will leave you.[2]

Action Step FC-6

Sometimes our lives get so cluttered that we have a hard time letting the Lord have control. This was true for Dian at one point in her life. She needed renewal, so she prayed something similar to the following, which you may also want to pray:

Lord,
I want You to renew my life and to bring me back to basics with You. Strip from me anything which is not from You and which is not absolutely necessary for our relationship. Later You can add anything You wish. I want to draw as close to You as possible, to be a person after Your own heart as David was. I want You to be first in my life.

If you were sincere in this prayer, you should find He will start changing you, taking away your desire for things you do not need right now, or at least giving you the ability to resist their attraction.

OBEDIENCE BRINGS FRUIT

As we let God's love touch our hearts more deeply, we will want to be more like He is. A good way to lay a firm foundation for such a step is through a study of the fruit of the Spirit.

Action Step FC-7

Do a personal study on the fruit of the Spirit. Galatians 5:22–23 states, "But the fruit of the Spirit is love, joy, peace, patience, kindness, goodness, faithfulness, gentleness and self-control. Against such things there is no law." So, how many fruits of the Spirit are there? If your answer is nine, look again. There is *one*—and this is very significant.

If a person believes that these verses describe "fruits" of the Spirit rather than the "fruit" of the Spirit, they will enjoy a freedom not designed in the Bible, a freedom to be picky about the fruit they want and the behavior they desire. But if we see all nine characteristics as a single unit, we will understand that God has described an all-round behavior which results from our direct relationship with our living Lord and trusted Companion.

Seeing the Lord Jesus as our constant Companion is to recognize a connection between root and fruit. If the roots go deeper, the fruits will ripen. Look at the scriptural connection of root and fruit in the eyes of faith:

Fruit	Character of God
Love	God is love (1 John 4:16).
Joy	He will rejoice over you (Zeph. 3:17).
Peace	The God of peace (Heb. 13:20).
Patience	He is patient with you (2 Pet. 3:9).

Kindness	He is kind to us (Eph. 2:7).
Goodness	I will see the goodness of the Lord (Ps. 27:13).
Faithfulness	Great is [His] faithfulness (Lam. 3:23).
Meekness	[Jesus is] meek and lowly (Matt. 11:29).
Self-Control	He has shown strength (Luke 1:51).

When you read a list like this, it is not hard to be over-whelmed. You may feel like the boy who became frustrated with his chicken who laid an egg that was much smaller than he had anticipated. He went to the store and returned home with a big bag. Kneeling down in front of the chicken, the boy pulled a large ostrich egg out of the bag. He held it in front of the unsuspecting fowl and said, "Take a good, long look . . . and try harder."

In a similar way, there is about as much a chance of a Christian demonstrating our Lord's divine example as there is of that chicken laying an ostrich egg. Nonetheless, we have to admit that there is a link between the fruit of the Spirit and the character of God as taught in Scripture. And Christians are expected to reproduce this unusual quality of life. Consider His directions:

Fruit	God's Standard for Us
Love	Love the Lord [and] your neighbor (Matt. 22:37–39).
Joy	Rejoice in the Lord (Phil. 4:4).
Peace	Seek peace and pursue it (1 Pet. 3:11).
Patience	Be patient with everyone (1 Thess. 5:14).
Kindness	Clothe yourself with kindness (Col. 3:12).
Goodness	Let us do good to all people (Gal. 6:10).
Faithfulness	Be faithful even to the point of death (Rev. 2:10).
Meekness	Show true meekness toward all men (Titus 3:2).
Self-control	Add to your knowledge, self-control (2 Pet. 1:5).

The fruit of the Spirit may be the result of inner workings of the Holy Spirit, but that does not mean human obedience and commitment is not involved. When we examine the fruit of the Spirit, we see a renewed role in the companionship of

God. To understand the fruit of the Spirit is to recognize our role in this relationship.

How close are you now to God? We would say at this level the relationship is the equivalent of hand in hand. It takes a definite act of the will to choose this deepening relationship. We must choose to be a companion of God and put our hand in His. There is an act of faith, trust, and submission in so doing.

YOUR HEART'S RESPONSE TO GOD

(Note: Write down on your "Area of Need" worksheet those areas of need you have yet to reach.)

A wise person once said, "When God measures you, He puts the tape around your heart, not your head." So how is your heart doing? As you have been going through the level of "Faithful Companion," the following should be happening:

- You should have a more intense desire to spend quality time with the Lord both in prayer and in the Word. Becoming a companion of the Lord will give you a hunger for the Word, in part, because that is how to get to know God better. Scripture will become an important resource through difficult situations as He leads you to specific promises to claim in each circumstance. Studying His Word will touch your emotions and give you a greater sense of His care and your security in Him.

The psalmist explained such a desire in Psalm 42:1: "As the deer pants for streams of water, so my soul pants for you, O God." Dian remembers reading that verse in 1981 and saying, "Lord, I know this should be true of me, but it is not. Yet I want it to be so. Please help me to feel this way, too." That prayer, along with several other circumstances and prayers, set her on the road to renewal in her own life.

Within a year's time she saw just such a change and hunger in her own life. Worship that used to seem strange to her no longer did. She was drawn to the older hymns of the church, seeing a beauty in them never before seen. Emotions that had been hidden by "proper worship" were now activated for the first time. She experienced a freedom of worship and expression of love for the Lord she had never had before. She knew what it meant to be "surprised by joy." The joy of the Lord became her inner strength and her delight.

As part of delighting in the Lord, there should be a corresponding delight in His Word. In Psalm 119 we read verse after verse of David's delight in the Word: "I delight in your decrees; I will not neglect your word. . . .Open my eyes that I may see wonderful things in your law. . . . My soul is consumed with longing for your laws at all times. . . .Your statutes are my delight; they are my counselors" (vv.16, 18, 20, 24).

Action Step FC-8

In a prayer similar to the following, ask the Lord to make these things true of you. (Note: If any part is not true for you, do not pray it; instead substitute anything appropriate to express your heart's desire.)

Father,

I want to know You so much better than I do, to have my feelings touched more by our relationship. I desire to have a hunger for Your Word and to understand it better. But at times I sense a block there. Help me not to give in to my flesh and procrastinate or find excuses not to spend time with You. Help me to put my relationship with You into a right perspective and to have a right balance between my physical life with all its demands and my spiritual life. Help me not to accept any enemy lies that the time I spend with You is a waste, or does not produce any results. Help me soon to reach that level of wanting to spend time with You simply because I love You so much, because I delight to be with You. Help my heart to truly delight in You. I have to admit right now, it is not at that point, but I really want

*it to be. Show me anything that may be interfering with
such a relationship with You. Help my emotions to catch up
with my heart and head's desires. Let my times with You
become interesting and productive.*

- You should find yourself more in love with God and in awe
  of who He is. You should want to please Him more and have
  a deeper understanding of His great love for you. Your heart
  and emotions should be touched at times as you think of
  your developing relationship with the Lord.

- You will become more submissive to God's will. This will be
  out of a heart of joy in submitting and not one of feeling
  obligated to submit. You will struggle less and less to submit
  to His leading because your trust in Him is growing. Your
  life will show His control in more areas, especially speech
  and actions.

- You will have a greater ability to praise God. Depending on
  your personality type, you may not find praise easy on the
  first three levels. But now, as God works in your life and
  heart, your emotions and desires should also be changing.
  Praising God will be more natural. You will not be offended
  by the praise of others, as you once may have been. You will
  learn new ways of praising Him. Words to songs that once
  were disdained—especially some of the old hymns of the
  faith—will come alive.

- The Word is more understandable. When you spend time
  with someone, you understand better what they say and
  how they think. This will be true for you as you read the
  Word. You are more sensitive to the Holy Spirit, actually
  wanting to hear Him speak to you, and therefore *listening*
  more intently.

- You will have a growing sense of the presence of God and
  His love and acceptance. One of the most gratifying things
  about growing closer to the Lord is the overwhelming,
  awesome sense of His presence both in good and bad times.

Companions do not have to make appointments to see each other; they are with each other all the time. You can almost "feel" Him there, walking beside you throughout your day, sharing the good, helping you through the bad. You can almost see Him smiling at you, guiding and encouraging you in what you are doing, pleased with your relationship. David talks about this close companionship in Psalm 23:4 when he says that the Lord, our Shepherd, walks beside us even when we go through the valley of the shadow of death.

- Your desire to draw closer to Him, to trust Him more and to please Him will intensify. Your heart will experience many emotions with the Lord, all of them positive. Among them will be an ever increasing desire to please Him, to be in the center of His will, to get as close to Him as possible.

- You will surrender most areas, yet you will still have some reservations about total commitment in certain areas. As much as you love the Lord, you will probably have some reservations in the deepest, most intimate, and important decisions of your life. You want to please the Lord and to do what He shows, but you still walk a little by sight and are not yet fully willing to do *whatever* He shows if you cannot *see* how it will turn out. You want things be logical first; in other words, you still walk by sight! At other times you do take some real leaps of faith. When you cannot quite bring yourself to take that leap, you will regress somewhat in the progress of drawing closer. As time goes on and you remain "soft clay in the potter's hand" (Isa. 64:8), you will be able to reach the stage of total commitment without sight.

THE MAIN FOCUS OF PRAYER

First, worship and praise will intensify. As we have already seen, drawing closer to God will impact our feelings about worship. Those drawing closer to God will find worship songs running through their mind more and more; the words of songs will touch their heart in a new way as they find these words expressing what they have been feeling.

Second, you should be moving in the direction of seeking God's agenda. One of the things a closer relationship with God produces is a greater sensitivity to what is on God's heart. This in turn creates a desire in our heart to see things more from His perspective. This leads to our praying that He will do that thing.

In chapter 1 we described the circle of prayer. This is what happens to the one who walks in companionship with the Lord.

Finally, prayer should be less of a struggle and more of a delight as one spends more time with the One they love.

Head knowledge has primarily been involved until now. But in reaching this level, head knowledge turns into heart experience. For some this will already be the case. But for others, heart knowledge is harder to experience. Once again, check yourself with chapter 2 to make certain all areas are covered so you can go on to level 5, Good Friend.

Action Step FC-9

Put on the "Armor of God" daily and check for any holes. See resource 8 . This will give both you and the enemy notice of how you want each day to be lived under God's absolute control. It will remind you of His role in defeating the enemy in every area of your life.

In Southern California, people try to survive to the weekend and the future hope of vacation. Imagine going on a vacation and deciding to take your goldfish with you for fear that it would die without your constant care. You would travel to the beach, enjoy the sun and the surf, but before long begin to feel guilty that the goldfish had not received the benefit of the vacation time. To make up for this injustice you might decide to take the goldfish out on your next beach day so your pet could enjoy life also.

So you would take the goldfish bowl with you the next day. When you reached the beach, you would take out your fishy companion from his bowl and lay him beside you on the towel. "Now my friend, here's your chance to enjoy all that I've been enjoying. Now, live it up!"

We laugh at how ridiculous this sounds because a fish has not been created by God to live in this kind of environment. It will surely die. It was never intended to be in this kind of situation. Neither are we. We were designed to enjoy a relationship with our Faithful Companion. He will never leave us alone and stranded on the sands of despair, for "He is with us."

◆

1 John 4:19.

2. James 4:7.

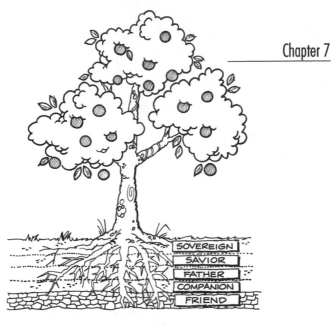

Chapter 7

Level 5
Good Friend

There is a friend who sticks closer than a brother.

PROVERBS 18:24

Action Step GF-1

*R*ead Ephesians and notice how Paul gives the believer a rich understanding of the scope of God's eternal purposes and blessings, along with His high standard for us. We suggest you continue to put what you find in the appropriate places in your journal.

There are some questions you can ask yourself that will help you think about what is being said. For example: "What does this mean to me and the way I live my daily life?" "Why is this important, especially to me?" "What am I to do about this information/standard/command? Is there a change I need to make?"

Action Step GF-2

These attributes and characteristics of God will become evident to anyone walking with Him in an intimate way: Great Wisdom, Perfection, Tough Love-Giver, Purity, Great Faithfulness, Gracious, Unselfish, Unchanging, Dependable, Unselfish, Warm-hearted. Make a sheet for each one along with any others you may want to investigate. Continue to meditate on these qualities of the Lord.

Few people have not been touched by the story of Helen Keller and her teacher Anne Sullivan as presented in the movie and play *The Miracle Worker*. Anne Sullivan was born half-blind, lost her mother at an early age, and ended up in the poor house. After surgery restored her sight at the Perkins Institute for the Blind, she devoted herself to the care of the blind. As a nineteen-month-old child, Helen Keller had lost both her hearing and her sight. When Helen was a young girl, Anne Sullivan became her teacher and taught her to spell by touching and spelling on her hands. Under her tutelage Helen Keller rose to renown. Teacher and pupil remained inseparable for forty-nine years.

The time came when misfortune befell Anne, who had since married and become Mrs. Macy. Her once-healed poor eyesight failed and she became blind. And now Helen Keller, her favorite student, became her teacher, helping her to overcome the lack of sight. Helen schooled her former teacher as devotedly as she herself had been schooled. Finally, Helen stood at the deathbed of her other half. When it was all over, Helen said these words: "I pray for strength to endure the silent dark until she smiles upon me again." This bond and oneness was the result of deep devotion, commitment, communication, and sincere friendship.

The following anonymous prayer clearly reflects the genuineness of a good friend:

Thank you, Lord, for giving me a friend whose special ways bring so much warmth and beauty to my heart, whose

gentleness and kindness brighten up so many days and make
so many happy moments start. Thank you, Lord, for giving
me a friend who's always there to cheer me anytime I feel low.
A friend who's glad to listen, really understands and cares,
who sees the best in me and helps me grow. A friend who
knows my hopes and fears and all I'm dreaming of, who's on
my side in everything I do. Thank you, Lord, for giving me
a friend so full of love . . . a friend who'll give me joy my
whole life through.

It sounds a lot like Anne Sullivan. But these qualities are also
found in a deepening relationship with God as you move
beyond seeing Him as Sovereign and Savior and Father and a
Faithful Companion, as your relationship progresses to that of
a Good Friend.

ESTABLISHING A BEACHHEAD

Glen has been called a Civil War fanatic. Whenever he travels
to places where there is a Civil War museum, battlefield, or gift
shop, he will be there.

There is a lot to learn about military tactics from reading
Civil War journals and history. One strategy was the establishing
of military command posts by "digging in." This same procedure was used in World War II as invading forces would likewise
"dig in" and establish what came to be known as a beachhead.
Once the beachhead was established, reinforcements would be
called in, additional supplies were shipped, and a process of
building up would take place despite the fact that they would
continue to encounter periodic counterattacks.

The problem with the beachhead format is found in its
initial vulnerability. Being compacted into a small area left the
soldiers particularly open, especially as the build up continued.
So at some point they had to reengage the enemy to test its
strength and to break through the confining perimeters of the
beachhead. The results would be more room to maneuver, more
real estate to build up, and continued stress on the enemy.

As you grow in your walk with God and the roots of understanding, fellowship, and intimacy dig deeper, you have in a sense established a beachhead. You have "built up" your understanding of God's attributes and have developed a deep sense of God as your heavenly Father and Companion. You find it much simpler to remain there, enjoy the benefits of the victories which you have attained, and rest. This is a status quo mentality—being comfortable where we are, with the problems we know and unwilling to venture into the unknown. This is why breaking through to the next level of Good Friend is often a struggle.

BREAKING THROUGH

Too many Christians spend the largest part of their lives in the "building up" process and rarely experience the remarkable freedom of breaking through. They have withstood the internal prompting of God's Spirit possibly precipitated by church attendance or Bible study. They have ignored a few of their friends who have gained the freedom of breaking through. They merely accept the status quo of life, never wanting to change or at least not willing to do what it takes to change. Probably the worst thing you could say to a growing Christian is, "You know, you haven't changed a bit." Have not changed? God is in you to work His good will and you have not changed? The Creator of the universe is offering every resource to you to be able to live for Him, and you have not changed?

Is it any wonder that throughout our nearly half-decade of combined ministry, we have heard people complain, "Why can't I grow? Where is my life headed? Why don't I have the peace and joy that so many other Christians have? What's wrong with me?" They have probably read how Christians are supposed to have "an inexpressible and glorious joy" (1 Pet. 1:8), but they have not yet begun to imagine the kind of Christian experience awaiting them in a friendship with the Lord in whom they have placed their faith and trust. Their experience would be more like "an inexpressible depression and life filled with worry."

There is no mystical formula for breaking through to the level of Good Friend. Numerous factors must all be taken into consideration. But one thing is certain: our personal and intimate relationship with the God of this universe is exciting and will produce significant spiritual benefits as our knowledge and intimacy grows. Let us suggest four benefits before we approach the action steps needed to break through to Good Friend.

First, you'll draw more on God's power. The Bible is very clear in declaring, "The people who know their God will display strength and take action" (Dan. 11:32, NASB). What a great promise! To know God is to become stronger, more powerful, and ready to take action. Why is this verse so important? To understand the verse, we must understand a little Jewish history. The Jewish people have faced many periods of intense persecution. Probably none of those trials was more devastating than a period under the tyranny of Antiochus Epiphanes, the Syrian king who reigned from 175 to 164 B.C. He changed his name to Theos Epiphanes, which means "the manifest God," but the Jewish people understood his real character when they changed one letter of his name and called him Epimanes, which meant "mad man." Certainly Antiochus Epiphanes was just that, a mad man, since he was literally insane with hatred for all Jews.

Daniel was a prophet. In the eleventh chapter of his book, Daniel predicted what course of events would take place under the leadership of Antiochus Epiphanes, and he was 100 percent accurate. Antiochus Epiphanes ordered Jewish sacrifices to stop, desecrated the temple with a "pig offering" on the altar, prohibited the observance of the Sabbath and the circumcision of children, set up idolatrous altars, and ordered all copies of the Scriptures to be destroyed. To disobey was to incur his wrath in the form of an ancient holocaust. How would the Jewish people ever survive this atrocity? Daniel knew: "The people who know their God will display strength and take action."

This is exactly what happened. A band of courageous men called the Maccabees led a heroic revolt against Antiochus. The odds were overwhelming; their exploits, nothing less than phenomenal. They knew their God, claimed His power, took action, and broke through the tyrannical stronghold of the enemy.[1] And people today who truly have a sense of God's presence and guidance have at their disposal the same degree of courage and power. There is no other way to gain this spiritual power except through an intimate knowledge of God.

Daniel himself knew His God intimately. When the leadership of the Medo-Persian Empire prevailed upon King Darius to issue a decree prohibiting anyone from praying to any god or man except for the king or be cast into the lions' den, Daniel continued to pray to the God of heaven (Dan. 6:4–15). He had no fear, because he knew God, and the people who know God will have the courage and strength to do His will despite the odds. As our knowledge of Him increases and our friendship with Him develops, He makes His power more readily available to us.

Second, you will discover peace. Peter explained a very important concept about people with a deepening relationship with God. He said, "Grace and peace be yours in abundance through the knowledge of God and of Jesus our Lord" (2 Pet. 1:2) This statement reveals that both grace and peace are ours in increasing amounts as we act on our increasing knowledge of God and our Savior. This peace is an inner tranquillity, a quiet confidence, an ability to stay under control in spite of the circumstances which may confront you. In a world seemingly coming apart at the seams, Christians who are drawing closer have a peace available. Therefore, we realize we have no reason to worry over every new problem.

The Book of Daniel gives another illustration of the peace that comes from knowing God as our Friend. King Nebuchadnezzar had just built a ninety-foot statue of himself before which every one of his subjects were commanded to bow. If anyone refused, death would be the result, by way of a fiery furnace. But three men—Shadrach, Meshach, and Abednego—were men who knew the living God as their Friend, so they would not bow down to this graven image. They made no defense for themselves but did what was right in the eyes of God. They even announced, "If we are thrown into the blazing furnace, the God we serve is able to save us from it, and he will rescue us from your hand, O king. But even if he does not, we want you to know, O king, that we will not serve your gods or worship the image of gold you have set up" (Dan. 3:17–18).

They knew without hesitation that their all-powerful God would deliver them. But even if He did not, it did not matter because they would be better off in His presence. They had perfect peace in the face of severe adversity.

Would you like this kind of peace? Would you like to stay relaxed in the face of trial or danger? This degree of peace depends upon your deepening relationship with God. As you know Him better and better, you sense His undying love and consistent presence, so you can relax even though storms rage all around you. From deep within will come that reassurance that "it is well with my soul." The peace of God brings a settledness to our minds which in turn gives us security and freedom from worry and fear. We can have peace that flows through our life as we walk in a secure relationship with God because we know He handles all our worries and cares.

Third, you'll discover wisdom. Paul was a man who enjoyed this benefit from knowing God. Paul often prayed that his followers would learn more about the advantages of a deeper walk with the Lord. For the people in Ephesus he prayed, "I keep asking that the God of our Lord Jesus Christ, the glorious Father, may give you the Spirit of wisdom and revelation, so that you may know him better" (Eph. 1:17) The word *spirit* is not a direct reference to the Holy Spirit, but rather a reference to a mental disposition of genuine spiritual understanding which can only come from the Holy Spirit. These Christians already had the indwelling Holy Spirit. Now Paul wanted them to grasp the spiritual realities available to them and appropriate these truths in their lives.[2]

Some people feel inadequate in spiritual understanding. They read the Word of God, but they have great difficulty understanding it or totally miss the appropriate application in their lives. Where is this spirit of wisdom to be found? Paul said in the knowledge of Him. The people who experience God as a Good Friend will have a deepening spiritual understanding despite their lack of theological training. The time they spend with Him will provide more insight and purpose of life than higher education could ever provide.

Peter and John were like that. They taught about Jesus and salvation in the temple courtyard one day and made the religious leadership very angry. The two were taken into custody and interrogated by the religious leaders, who demanded to know where they received their power to do miracles. Peter was the first to speak as usual. He delivered a powerful testimony of the person of Jesus Christ and demonstrated his familiarity with the Old Testament Scriptures (Acts 4:8–12). All of this from an uneducated fisherman? Yes, because Peter had been with the Lord (Acts 4:13).

The Jewish leaders could see that Peter's relationship was not a shallow one. It was an ever-growing, ever-deepening walk with Christ. The religious leaders with all their theological training were no match for Peter because people who know God as a Friend have His wisdom and have the mind of Christ.

Fourth, you will discover growth. One of our favorite passages is Paul's prayer for the people in the Colossian church where he describes another advantage of knowing God: "For this reason, since the day we heard about you, we have not stopped praying for you and asking God to fill you with the knowledge of his will through all spiritual wisdom and understanding. And we pray this in order that you may live a life worthy of the Lord and may please him in every way: bearing fruit in every good work, growing in the knowledge of God" (Col. 1:9–10). Do you understand what Paul has said? The knowledge of God is the means by which we bear fruit and increase in every good work God wants us to accomplish.

The knowledge of God empowers us to bear fruit and do what He wants us to do. Have you ever said, "Why can't I do what's right?" or "Why don't I enjoy the love and joy that others experience in their Christian walk?" One reason might be the lack of depth in your relationship with the Lord.

We need not only knowledge about the truths of the Bible, but also perspective in our understanding of why God does what He does. When you grow in your knowledge of friends, you enjoy being with them more and desire to please them more. This is exactly what happens in our relationship with Jesus. The more we know of His love for us, the more we will love Him in return. As John wrote in 1 John 4:19: "We love because he first loved us."

Consider the following analogy. Psychologists tell us that we develope similarities to the people with whom we are the closest. Likewise, as we spend more time with our Savior, grow in our knowledge of Him, and develop Christlikeness,[3] we will bear fruit and good works because of our knowledge and intimacy with God. The closer we are to Him, the more we will enjoy our spiritual experience and the more we will grow in our relationship with Jesus. This is the ultimate goal of our life: to be like Jesus. This is one of the key reasons God has left us here on earth.[4]

SEEKING THIS DIVINELY ORDAINED FRIENDSHIP

The word *friendship* initiates a variety of mental pictures. But despite the diversity of opinion regarding what real friendship is all about, certain common denominators are vital to its growth and continued viability. In our friendship-relationship with God, the same is true. Let us look at those action steps needed for this friendship to flourish.

Action Step GF-3

Live a lifestyle of confession. If these are your thoughts, be willing to pray the following:

God,

I admit that I am not You. And I do not even need to apply for the job, because there is no vacancy in the Trinity. You are not finished with me yet and I must submit myself to the changes You want to bring about in my life and the holiness You expect if I am ever going to be able to enjoy a close friendship with You.

Is confession simply a recitation of all your inadequacies and insufficiencies? Is it merely the displaying of a person's dirty laundry for everyone else to examine and critique? No, confession is much more than that.

David knew the importance of confession. He saw it as the opportunity to examine who was really in charge and to initiate a marvelous change of perspective in his life.

David wrote in Psalm 139:1–4, 23–24:

> O LORD, you have searched me and you know me. You know when I sit and when I rise; you perceive my thoughts from afar. You discern my going out and my lying down; you are familiar with my ways. Before a word is on my tongue you know it completely, O LORD. . . .Search me, O God, and know my heart; test me and know my anxious thoughts. See if there is any offensive way in me, and lead me in the way everlasting.

What changes are necessary in your life? What dynamics of relationship should be true as you enter this Good Friend level?

Reason for Obedience

Obedience will be based on a *deep love for God* and a *desire to do His will.* Submission to His will usually will be seen as desirable because of the deep-seated trust that has developed. Tithing and giving of gifts to the Lord will become a way of life. You will seek out ways to give to God and His people.

Degrees of Closeness

The *closeness* you experience with God will be like being *arm in arm*. Good friends always want to touch and are often linked arm in arm as they walk along. It would be impossible for two, linked arm in arm, to walk with much distance between them or to go in different directions. There definitely is agreement, and since the Lord cannot walk a wrong road, we are walking His road.[5]

Your Heart's Response

Your heart's response to God will be one of greatest joy to have the opportunity to know and serve Him.

First, much of the fear the enemy has thrown at you to make you mistrust God should be gone. You should also sense a strong drawing toward Him—a deep desire to be with Him, and to have the privilege of serving Him. Before you may have served Him although at times you felt it was an imposition. Now you consider service a privilege. Whatever He asks, you will want to do. On rare occasions you may have a reservation about what He says. You may hesitate as you mull over the desirability of doing this difficult thing He asks of you. This is one of the key differences between this level and the next. At the Good Friend level you may still *reserve the right to make a decision on everything God asks you to do. You still may choose to have "rights."*

Those at the Intimate Level trust God so much that they have given up all "rights" and are willing to do whatever He asks, knowing in full faith He is worthy of their trust and would never ask them to do anything that was not the best thing for them. They have chosen to walk fully by faith and not by sight. In contrast is the Good Friend level where people walk by sight through their own mind's ability to evaluate each request, to weigh the consequences and only then to decide if they are going to do what God has asked.

We can compare this to the question of where self is when Jesus is in control of the life. Picture an old fashioned scale with two dishes suspended between the cross arms. In the dish on the right side is God's will for my life. On the left, with equal weight, is a competing will for my life—something I want to do, something the enemy of my soul wants me to do.

For many, self is to the side, but not out of the picture. Each time a decision is necessary, self will weigh the pros and cons and almost always come down on the side of God's will. But once in a while self will decide it wants to go on the left side. However, for the Intimate Level self will be a permanent resident on the right side—God's side—no matter what is put on that side. There is never a decision to make—only the need to know which side God is on so self can do whatever He asks. We will discuss this more in chapter 8.

Sometimes in our walk with the Lord, as He asks us to do something we have resisted doing for ever so long, we can decide to give in, but in so doing we can also get angry with God and pull back, even though we obeyed.

Dian recalls counseling with Julie who had struggled with God about a certain issue. "Why don't you turn it over to Me?" was God's persistent encouragement to her. Finally, in anger, she did so. But at the same time she told God, "I'll never again submit to You by force. You've got this life, but that's all. I'm fed up with having to walk the straight and narrow, doing exactly what You want. I have a right to make my own decisions without You forcing me to do something that I really think is unfair."

As Dian listened, she saw the results such an attitude had on this person with such potential, yet misery. She was ready to give her life back to God, but she still wanted to hold on to a few areas. As Julie put it, "There are certain sensitive areas of my life where I am unwilling to trust Him fully." Why? The answer was simple. Julie had been willing to trust God with all areas she did not want to control, where she felt she needed help. But she could not turn over "personal" areas, the ones she wanted to control. But this was the very thing God was gently yet firmly asking her to turn over to Him—her desire for control.

This is a very difficult thing for all of us to do. Our inborn desire to control can be seen from the cradle as the baby demands to be fed and changed when *it* wants, not when we want. Later in the terrible two's we see more control expressed through temper tantrums. Some children learn to control by being cute or charming; others through disobedience. At each level of physical maturity, areas need to be surrendered to someone else's control. Usually this is done because the person is smaller or weaker than the authority figure. But when adulthood is finally reached, many individuals want to throw off all restraints and take control of every area of their lives. Some never stop this process and rebel against their bosses, the law, and God.

Action Step GF-4

When God shows you something to do, is your response anything like the following? "What do *I* want? Will this fit in with how *I* want my life to be? Is this something that will help *me* reach my goals? Fit in with *my* ambition? Do I really trust Him with *this* area?" Do your answers show that you are more concerned about what you want than what God wants? If so, you need to recognize that your life is not yielded fully to the Lord.

People who want to keep control of their life and only follow God in those areas that make sense to them or fit their desires are not walking in submission to the Lord. Pride in one's own plans and abilities and wanting to see the end before starting down a road are all the world's ways of doing things, not the Lord's. He wants faith and trust.

Pride in your own ability to understand things conflicts with the Lord, whose ways are not your ways. He will always win. This is why Lloyd Ogilvie uses this description: "We become a walking civil war."[6]

Second, as you walk closer with God, you will experience a stripping away of unsuitable areas of life. You may obey His requests, but often you struggle before submitting completely.

Third, another change you will notice is that the Scriptures are more alive and "sweeter" to you. You will have a definite desire to get into them regularly. David experienced the delight one has in reading the Word. "How sweet are your promises to my taste, sweeter than honey to my mouth!" (Ps. 119:103). As with any friend, we delight to hear them talk, to share their heart, to learn the things they care about, and to get their insights on the things that concern you.

Dian recalls when she prayed something similar to the one in the next action step. At the time the Lord was just beginning to work renewal in her life. After saying this simple prayer, she found herself very eager to get to her quiet time and anxious to see what the Lord would show her that morning. She looked forward to what He would put His finger on through the Word and because of it remove something else that was not compatible with being like Jesus.

She recalls, "Each morning I knew He would show me something and that I would have to deal with it. I surprised myself at how, as an independent person, I eagerly looked forward to being told I needed to change something in my life. The thought that kept running through my head was, 'Yes, He will show something that is less than perfect, but this will be something in my life that is dross[7] and needs to be removed so I can be more like Jesus and be a "person after God's own heart."'[8]

What we come to realize in our close walk with the Lord is that to be a person after God's own heart is to be a person *with* the heart of God. This can only come as we spend significant, meaningful times with Him, walking, talking in intimacy, sharing everything.

Action Step GF-5

As you read the above, you may feel this is not where your heart is, even though you are at the Good Friend level. You may have wondered why you hesitate when the Holy Spirit talks to you about this problem. One reason for many who are drawing closer to the Lord is that they may have drawn closer through prayer more than through the study of the Word. Prayer is conversation and can be done at any time. Studying the Word takes time and effort.

Believers may know the Word is important, read it, learn, and at times become excited by what they read. But they may find they have *no real attraction* to the Word; it is more like their daily spiritual vitamin pill to stay healthy. They appreciate how it impacts their life, and would not think of missing its input, but they do not consider God's words "honey" to them. If you find yourself identifying with this scenario, then the following prayer may be of help:

Lord,

I read Job and David's thoughts about how sweet Your words were to them; how much they desired them more than even their food.[9] Father, I like food. I desire it very much. But my heart does not respond that way to Your words. I wish it did, for I want it to. Please help me feel such an attraction to Your Word. I want to be touched emotionally by the desire to daily read Your love letter to me, Your instructions, and to daily see new and wonderful things You have in it for me. Help me prioritize my time, too, so I can be in Your Word more without feeling the pressure of time constraints. I want to savor it as I would a wonderful meal. Let me feast on Your Word. Draw me to the banquet table of Your Word. Then help me to "meditate on it all day long."[10] Help me to see it as wonderful, not oppressive or burdensome.[11]

Remember, meditation is like digesting food. It helps to process what has been taken in and apply it to the appropriate part of your spiritual life. It also builds up reserves so you have some nourishment and strength when you need it. And remember, you know how to meditate—you already do it when you worry, constantly dwelling on a subject, thinking about it from every angle. Now use this skill in a constructive way, a godly way to analyze and digest the Word.

Fourth, a natural outflow of reading the Word from a fresh perspective is deepening praise and worship. Scripture provides a rich source for both. In addition, songs that once were humdrum should now seem more meaningful and touch your heart in a fresh way. If this is not happening you may want to pray a prayer like the following:

> *Father,*
>
> *I feel so inadequate in my worship of You. You are so wonderful and awesome and I love You so much; but I usually have a hard time knowing how to worship You as You should be. I really want to feel like praising and worshiping you. I would love to be able to raise my voice in meaningful praise and lift my hands in adoration without feeling self-conscious or that I am being a hypocrite. In general I desire to have a lot more freedom and variety in my worship. Show me how to do this. Teach my heart how not to be self-conscious. Make it flow from deep within me, affecting every part of my being so that I worship You as fully and thoroughly as You deserve.*

Recently we read this simple, yet profound definition of worship: "The simple pleasure of looking at the one you love is what we enjoy each time we worship God and bask in His presence."[12]

Fifth, you will also find as you reach this level of relationship that wanting what pleases God is more important to you than your own desires. At times you will willingly set aside your plans to do something God asks you to do. There may be a little regret, but there will be obedience. In the next level, most, if not all, regret will be gone.

Sixth, these results have come because your roots have gone very deep into the Lord. You will be living and operating more and more from biblical standards, rather than the world's. This may have happened even in a previous level, but it certainly will be a way of life by this level.

Finally, your faith will be strong to the point others cannot easily pull you away from what God wants you to do or think, even though your trust may not be quite as strong. Therefore, only a few things may still be withheld from unconditional surrender.

Main Focus of Prayer

Your main focus of prayer will be in spending quality time with the Lord, in increased sensitivity to His voice, and in becoming more God-centered in your desires.

You will spend more and more quality time with the Lord both in prayer and Bible study. This will be very important to you, even to the point of being willing to sacrifice sleep time. Many people at this level get up at 4:30 a.m. to have an uninterrupted time with the Lord. They want to start their day out strongly with the Lord and not have to worry about the clock. Of course, this also means getting to bed earlier the night before so you will be alert when you get up. When relationship becomes a high enough priority, time is made to spend with the One you care about.

If this is a problem for you or you are not a morning person, you will probably benefit from reading some of our suggestions in our book *Power House* about how to handle this in an effective way. As part of that book, we have a number of good resources. Resources 1 and 2 on drawing closer and the two-week enrichment plan for drawing closer to the Lord in your quiet time would be excellent to follow.

We also have prayers centered around your family, the church, and specific needs such as praying for a difficult person, praying the Scriptures, how to pray for character qualities in one's life, etc. *Power House* also includes a very good nine-page annotated bibliography of books, tapes, and other resources on prayer and Bible study. One book mentioned that is excellent is the Henry Blackaby and Claude V. King workbook on *Experiencing God.*

You will pray for increased sensitivity to the voice of God. As the world becomes less important and things do not crowd out your time with the Lord as much as they used to, you will find yourself better understanding what He desires to communicate to you. The Word will become more alive and relevant in speaking to concerns, as you will recall Scriptures that will answer your questions. You will find pertinent articles or radio/TV programs which the Spirit will lead or in many other ways find you are constantly understanding the leading and communication of the Lord. As part of this process you will also be able to distinguish more and more between His voice and that of the enemy or your own fallen humanity's desires.

Prayer will become more God-centered as your desires are conformed to what God wants.

Effect of Your Relationship with God on Others

You may find people seeking your advice because of your walk with the Lord and resulting wisdom. To you the things you believe and advise others are just common sense, yet they are biblically based because the Word is strong in you. Be careful not to let this puff you up! Walk in humility as others come to you for advice and you find your counsel accepted and used by people to solve their problems God's way.

There should be a strong desire to walk free of sin. It is hard to be close to those we have offended. We want to please our friends. As you grow ever closer with your Good Friend, you will not want to do anything that may grieve Him or be against His will. Therefore, You will deal with sin quickly.

You will go the extra mile to maintain a Christ-honoring relationship with others who may be difficult. This means you will forgive easily, even though you may be saddened or hurt by the actions of the person. You will never hold grudges for that would break your fellowship with the Lord. If you start to do so, the conviction of the Holy Spirit will bring you back to the right attitude.

Outlook on Life

There will be a deepening peacefulness in your life no matter what the circumstance. Your faith and trust in God will always intercept the fiery darts of doubt and fear the enemy tries to throw your way when circumstances are not good.

Although you may recognize your weaknesses and have not yet fully corrected them, you will desire to do so, and you feel confident the Lord will help you. You will be regularly seeking His help in overcoming shortcomings.

Even though we said the following in the overview for chapter 1, it bears repeating here. The difference between Good Friend and Intimate Friend for the individual is a fine line. It basically is the degree of trust, faith, commitment, and surrender. Some people cross this line quickly, others take more time. The Good Friend relationship is one which always reserves the right to say no. The Intimate Friend has come to the point of absolute surrender because he or she is so convinced of the goodness and sovereignty of God that trust is there no matter what their human feelings may be.

As you prepare for the final level, it is good to bear the following in mind. Sometimes we say we want to draw closer to God and yet are not willing to do the things necessary to be there. We need to be honest in all we do—not that we will be perfect, but rather that we will always have as our goal to do the right thing which is what the Lord shows us to do. Here are three questions we ask ourselves to evaluate things in our lives to see if they fit God's standards. You could have many more, and probably should, as God shows you specific things for your life.

Is it edifying? A PG movie on TV starred a well-liked actress, yet the theme was about a prostitute and one of her clients. Since this was not edifying, there was no struggle with the decision.

The verse in Philippians 4:8 becomes the standard: "Whatever is true, whatever is noble, whatever is right, whatever is pure, whatever is lovely, whatever is admirable—if anything is excellent or praiseworthy—think about such things." For the television you may add Psalm 101:3: "I will set before my eyes no vile thing."

Is this compromising to the world's standards or a form of rationalization? Southern California usually has very lax enforcement of speeding laws. Normal traffic flow will stay at 60–63 miles an hour, with some cars going 70–90. When traveling on the freeway and tempted to speed, Dian reminds herself that just because everyone else is breaking the 55 mph law does not give her permission to do so. Which is *not* to say she does not do it at times, but she does not rationalize and say, "Everyone's doing it, so therefore it is all right for me to do so."

Dian's brother, David, taught her this lesson. He said that if he, as a youth leader, sped, then he could not blame his kids when they chose to break the law, either in driving or another area. To make his point more fun for the kids, he told them that he always knew when he was going too fast because he could see the hood of his car raise about an inch. Why? His guardian angels could not protect him when he was breaking the law and had to jump off at 55 mph!

The world is so clever in compromising on what God has set up as the standard. We can rationalize so easily, because to do so satisfies our fallen nature's world view—a view that says, "Whatever benefits/satisfies/pleases me is what I will do, no matter what other factors there may be. I'm the only one that counts. I have to look out for number one."

How are my emotions responding? A few years ago Dian noticed that every time she looked at a picture of one of her family members, she felt negatively toward him. A year or so before there had been some misunderstandings, which had been worked out. She had felt he had not believed the truth in a certain thing, and that had hurt. So, even though they had talked things out and forgiven each other, she realized that obviously she still carried the hurt. Her immediate response was to ask the Lord to take the hurt and give her back the loving feeling she truly had for him. And it worked!

At this point, you will want to go back to the quiz and see if you are ready for the Intimate Level. If you determine you are, come and experience a high level of intimacy with your beloved Lord and God. This level is unlike any other, for it is similar to the one we will walk in heaven. It is a level that never ends in its discoveries of the joys of our Lord. Jesus says this is what happens to those who are faithful with what He has put into their hands: "Come and share your master's happiness!" (Matt. 25:21).

This story is told of Shah Abbis, a Persian monarch who loved his people very much. To know and understand them better, he would mingle with his subjects in various disguises.

One day, disguised as a poor man, he went to the public baths. In a tiny cellar, he sat beside the fireman who tended the furnace. When it was mealtime, the monarch shared this man's coarse food and talked to this lonely subject as a friend.

Again and again he visited and the man grew to love the monarch without figuring out who he was. One day the Shah told him he was the monarch, expecting the man to ask for some gift from him.

But the fireman sat gazing at the ruler with love and wonder and at last spoke, "You left your palace and your glory to sit with me in this dark place, to eat of my coarse food, to care whether my heart was glad or sorry. On others you may bestow rich presents, but to me you have given yourself, and it only remains for me to pray that you will never withdraw the gift of your friendship."

How unlike most people today. Yet having reached this level of relationship with his monarch, this peasant did not want to gain personal benefit such as gifts. He wanted the monarch for who he was. So it should be with our relationship with the Lord.

We should want Him for who He is, not what He can do for us or give us or make us into.

Did you notice? This man experienced the rich rewards of friendship with his ruler, yet as great as that was, he knew there was no guarantee this was a permanent relationship.

But how different it is for us as we walk with the One who is King of kings and Lord of lords—and yet our Good Friend. He wants to walk in intimacy with us eternally. He chose to draw us closer to Him and says nothing will separate us from Him. He may correct us on occasion, but He never breaks the relationship. We are His children and He loves us. What a secure place to be! But there is even more, so you will want to go on, to draw closer in the final step.

◆

1. For a concise discussion on the exploits of King Antiochus IV and the revolt led by the Maccabees, see Werner Keller, *The Bible as History* (New York: Bantom Books, 1965), 347–52.

2. See discussion of Ephesians 1:17 in Frank E. Gaebelein, ed., *The Expositor's Bible Commentary*, vol. 11 (Grand Rapids, Mich.: Zondervan, 1978), 29–30.

3. 2 Corinthians 3:18.

4. See Romans 13:14; 1 Corinthians 1:30.

5. See Amos 3:3.

6. Lloyd Ogilvie, 32.

7. Isaiah 48:10; Zechariah 13:9.

8. Acts 13:22.

9. Job 23:12.

10. Psalm 119:97.

11. Psalm 119:35, 129.

12. Greg Asimakoupoulos, *Leadership Magazine* (Winter 94), 47.

13. Henry Blackaby and Claude V. King, *Experiencing God: Knowing and Doing the Will of God* (Nashville, Tenn.: LifeWay Press, 1990). Broadman and Holman also has a trade book, *Experiencing God: How to Live the Full Adventure of Knowing and Doing the Will of God* by Henry T. Blackaby and Claude V. King. See your nearest Christian bookstore.

14. Matthew 25:21,23.

15. See Romans 8:35–38.

Chapter 8

SOVEREIGN
SAVIOR
FATHER
COMPANION
FRIEND
INTIMATE FRIEND

Level 6:

Intimate Friend

I have called you friends, for everything that I learned from my Father I have made known to you.

JOHN 15:15

Action Step IF-1

*S*tart reading Proverbs. This book is rich with wisdom. Pray before you start each day that the Lord will teach you to be wise. Continue to put what you find in the appropriate places in your journal. Proverbs will supply you with new ideas to enter in your "Area to Work on" section.

Action Step IF-2

The following attributes and characteristics will be very important to focus on for anyone walking with the Lord in an intimate way: Tenderhearted, Gentleness, Great Heart of Love, Complete Ability to Meet Every Need and Care, Absolute Sovereign, Absolute Control, Totally Good, Wants the Very Best for Me, and Is Committed to Me. Make a sheet for each one along with any others you may want to investigate. Continue to meditate on these qualities of the Lord.

Every child loves change. One reason is that children equate change with growth which is not a bad assumption. On one occasion, Glen's middle child, Scott, came into the living room explaining how much he had grown in the past week. Evidently the growth chart had fallen to the ground and his sister Kerry had hung it back up without checking to see if it had been replaced correctly. Scott was now just under five feet tall as a ten-year-old. As carefully and tactfully as possible, Glen and Nancy tried to explain that this was impossible and went back to where the chart was hanging to correct the measurement standards. Since Kerry hung the chart improperly, Scott had made incorrect measurements and was many inches off.

Many Christians make very similar mistakes in gauging their spiritual growth and maturity by incorrect standards. Compared to a shortened scale or an inferior standard, we can appear further along than we actually are. Only when we stand at the feet of Jesus, the ultimate standard, do we ever discover how far we have to go. Since He is willing to help us and be with us always as our Intimate Friend, we can begin to understand what level 6 is all about.

SEEING GOD AS AN INTIMATE FRIEND

We have achieved our heart's desire. We have reached our destination—the Intimate Friend level. This level should never end. It is as though we have waited for our wedding day, and now it is here!

Our hearts are prepared, eagerly anticipating walking in intimate friendship with our God. Our time with Him until now has had some wonderful foretastes of this, but now it is a reality. Enoch walked and talked with God. Abraham was a friend of God. David was a man after God's own heart. Moses talked with God face to face. And I, I too am an intimate friend of God's.

It no longer is theory but experience. It is faith not sight. I am His and He is mine. I am in awe of who He is, what He is, and who I am to Him. I am overwhelmed and humbled with my heart bowing in adoration and appreciation.

For those reading the above who have yet to reach this level, the words may sound flowery, silly, or too much like emotional hype. But to the heart that is experiencing their reality, these words are weak and incapable of catching the thrill, the joy, the pleasure of having such a close fellowship with the Lord. To them this is their usual experience to one degree or another.

We often compare it to being color blind, seeing only in black and white with tones of gray versus being able to see all the many brilliant colors and their blends of shades. Viewing a sunset can be a totally different experience for those who see color and those who do not. They all see the same sky, but one group experiences a richer, deeper, more exciting quality to the view. Those in the other group can appreciate that there is something there. But unless they see color, they will never truly understand or fully appreciate all that God has created for humans to enjoy.

Our culture uses many different ways to explain the word *intimacy*. Apart from its sexual connotation, we use it in such statements as "an intimate dinner for two," or a close, memorable dinner. When we talk about an intimate friendship, we are usually indicating a close, deep relationship. When we use it with God, we are talking about a closeness that is wed with understanding, confidence, and total acceptance. There is a growing knowledge and appreciation associated with intimacy with Him, a joy from knowing Him in a special way. Such a relationship cannot be matched by any other human friendship. It is unique with God, one to which we were created and have a longing for when our hearts are right before Him.

Action Step IF-3

Go back over those qualities of God listed in chapters 3 to 7 and see what new insights you can add to each one. Sometimes we take things for granted because they have become so familiar to us. Certainly God is great, but what does that mean, especially now that we have walked with Him for some time and have gotten to see many examples of His greatness? To avoid familiarity creating an insensitivity to the awesome God we love and serve, we suggest you ask yourself about the interdependency of each characteristic on the other. How great does it make our God that He has each of these qualities? How would you feel if He were missing any of them? Why? Which ones thrill you the most and why? Which ones seem the least important?

Action Step IF-4

Take the questions from the above exercise that seem least important and ask God to show you more about them to help you appreciate Him more for this particular aspect of His nature. Write down what He unfolds of Himself to you. To appreciate His faithfulness, you might want to date each entry so that you see the progressive way He reveals Himself to your understanding. Another helpful entry would be to record your own heart's response to this new piece of information about God, this new piece of the God-puzzle He has given you.

You will discover that you will never exhaust the new things you are learning about your Intimate Friend. He is so far above us that we will never plumb the depths of all He is. And that is wonderful. We never get bored with our wonderful Lord.

Action Step IF-5

Any ship that is sailing from one point to a specific destination periodically needs to take a mid-course fix on their position and make any necessary adjustments. In our spiritual life, the same is true. Our goal is to walk with the Lord in a close relationship that you maintain until we go Home. But sometimes we get off on some subtle, almost parallel side roads if we are not careful.

Now that you have gone over the above questions, there is one very important one to ask: Am I giving Him all the respect He deserves because of who He is? In other words, am I too casual in our relationship because we have become so close? Am I presumptuous, expecting Him always to say yes simply because we are such good friends? Meditate on the answer, and then deal with whatever you find needs correction.

Action Step IF-6

Take inventory by asking this question: How do my values compare to God's? Use your notes from Psalms and Proverbs and your "Areas to Work on" sheets as a starting point. Then read Galatians 4:19, 5:19–6:3; Ephesians 4:1–3, 4:22–6:4; and the Book of Philippians. Ask God to show you what He wants you to do about those areas that are weak. Then do it!

In the third chapter of Revelation, Jesus makes some definitive statements concerning the Laodicean church. Everyone who is responsible for some aspect of God's work must come to terms with the responsibility. On one occasion, Glen spent an entire week looking at the work he was doing as a pastor. He made a list of everything he typically tried to accomplish in a week, and beside the list he rated each event as to comparative value in light of eternity. He found that a great deal of his regular schedule had little or no discernible value in these terms.

What really blesses you? What upsets you? What do you worry about? If you lie awake sleepless, what is it that keeps you awake? In other words, what are your values?

In general, we are probably the best equipped bunch of professing Christians that ever came down the path of history. We have all the gadgets and equipment and more money per capita than most of the people who have gone before us, yet society, again in general, still reaches for more. What are the real values? The priorities will always determine the procedure. Whatever you determine most important determines what you will do and, more importantly, when you will do it. Priorities determine which way our feet are facing and also whether or not we are getting the job done. It is easy to get so busy doing a lot of things that we fail to grapple with the pressing issues and heartaches that ought to be settled. Stewardship of time, talents, and treasures will always follow values.

Those who are at an Intimate Friend level have a strong desire that what they do makes some contribution to the Kingdom. This becomes a priority of their stewardship. They will be more focused on what counts for eternity than on the short-lived pleasures of today. They have experienced the truth of Jesus' admonition that if we seek first the kingdom of God and His righteousness, then all our earthly needs will be met. That does not mean they have to go into full-time Christian work. Some of God's most productive workers are the Marys and Marthas who are at home, the ones in the business world who influence their colleagues for the Lord, and the ones who spend time with their families, attend school functions, teach Sunday School, serve on church leadership boards, sing in the choir, do AWANA or whatever other personal ministry the Lord has given them.

Jesus had more appreciation for the average person than those who were wealthy, well known, or in prestigious positions. Just read the Sermon on the Mount to see His blessings on "the poor in spirit," and "the meek."[1] He was not impressed with people in power, but rather chose fishermen, tax collectors—nobodies—to be in His inner circle of friends. He loved associating and eating with the poor, the despised, the outcasts.

Action Step IF-7

Reset your priorities. If you want to find out what is really important, ask yourself what someone else should complete if you died suddenly, and you will easily know. Some things just can wait; other things ought not to wait. The priorities of the Christian life have a definite bearing on how much intimacy we are going to have with God. Once we have placed our priorities under God, some things have to go.

As we have mentioned in other contexts, You will have an absolute sense of His presence and friendship at all times and a desire to live a squeaky clean life, so that even the hint of anything that might be slightly outside the will of the Lord, or be even questionable, is rejected. Persons at this level will ask themselves any time they hesitate about whether or not they should do something, "Is it squeaky clean?" This will normally settle the answer one way or another. In other words, in an Intimate Friend relationship, we purposely choose to set aside our right to rationalize or give excuses for why we should do something. If it is questionable, it is out of bounds. This is done out of a heart of love for the Lord that wants to do nothing to grieve or disappoint Him. Little things that once were overlooked, ignored, or compromised are no longer tolerated.

In chapter 7 we showed you how to "strip" everything from your life that was blocking your relationship with the Lord. Have you done that? Are there new things that need to be added? You might want to ask yourself: What does God have to say about this? What counts for eternity? What are my goals, and does this help me reach them? This matter of good stewardship follows a kind of holy desperation that says, "God told me to do this and I have to do it."

Hearing this commitment, you cannot help but remember a prophet by the name of Amos in the Bible. He traveled miles to reach the king's court and made his way into the courtroom where he began to preach about pending wrath coming to Bethel. A priest named Amaziah stopped him and said, "Get out, you seer! Go back to the land of Judah. Earn your bread there and do your prophesying there. Don't prophesy anymore at Bethel, because this is the king's sanctuary and the temple of the kingdom" (Amos 7:12–13). Amos did not hesitate. He said, "I was neither a prophet nor a prophet's son, but I was a shepherd, and I also took care of sycamore-fig trees. But the LORD took me from tending the flock and said to me, 'Go, prophesy to my people Israel.' Now then, hear the word of the LORD," (Amos 7:14–16). What was Amos' authority? How could he be so bold? Because God had told him to do this and he had to do it. Priorities!

The apostle Paul lived in a day and age when it may have been fatal to be a Christian. A citizen had few rights, even a Roman citizen, if it became known he or she was a follower of Jesus Christ. Paul must have been under a lot of pressure. On his way to Jerusalem, the Holy Spirit had actually warned him to expect problems and even imprisonment. He was going straight into trouble with pressures from outside and pressures from within the church. Despite the warnings of leadership, Paul decided to go. Therefore the believers could boldly proclaim, "The Lord's will be done" (Acts 21:14).

For it is not what we are doing now that is important, it is how we are going to end that is! Find a person who has decided the priorities of life and follows those priorities, and you will see others that are willing to follow. People who are committed to do what God has called them to do will never lack for followers.

Action Step IF-8

Get in business with God. Who is in control in your life? You or God? By now you should without hesitation respond, "God." How much do you trust Him—*really* trust Him? If you mean real business with God, if you trust that He wants only the best for you and that you can depend upon Him no matter what He asks of you, then one way of expressing this is to do the following: Take a blank sheet of paper and write at the top the date and the word "CONTRACT" in the center. Then write this note: "Dear Father, I love You and trust You with every area of my life. Do with it as You wish. Fill in the rest of this page with whatever You want for my life, and I will do it." Finally, sign your name at the bottom with the date.

Our experience is that when you do this, or contemplate doing it, you may find yourself in a battle of the mind with many reasons why you should not do this. *This is crazy. Who knows what God may ask of you!! You're opening up the door for Him to send you to Africa, make you marry a "dog," get you in a bad accident, take away your security, give you cancer or AIDS. You'd better not do this. It is way too risky. Let God show you what He wants first, then you can decide whether or not to do it. That is the safest way. Don't do something dumb you'll regret for the rest of your life. It's just not worth it. After all, if you sign this and He then asks something weird of you, you're stuck. You're a person of integrity and won't go back on your word. So don't sign it in the first place. Then you won't have to worry all the time what may be asked of you.*

Such thoughts go with the drawing closer process. You need to recognize and sort out what is temptation and what is from your own flesh. If your heart's desire is to do a certain thing and these negative thoughts flood your mind—and your response is, "I can trust God no matter what. I want to do this"—then you are ready to take this step. If you are having reservations that you truly feel are from you—ones you have yet to deal with and which have probably been part of your hesitations in the past—then you need to determine which reservations are legitimate and find the answers before following any course. Involve the Lord in your search.

Action Step IF-9

Sharpen your decision-making skills. As we have just seen, you may come to the point where there is something you want to do, but at the same time you truly have some questions about it. How can you determine if it is Satan's attack, maybe using a weakness of your flesh, or in fact a true check of the Holy Spirit? The following questions are designed to help you identify the source(s). Recognize that there may be more than one source. Your flesh is always a prime candidate, but often Satan will intensify already existing weaknesses of the flesh. His attacks are harsh and depressing, whereas the Holy Spirit will be gentle and persistent and show you God's truth as part of the solution. The same decision may have input from all three sources, which can make it even more confusing. So you need to sort through everything carefully if you are to avoid misunderstanding what God wants you to do or avoid.

- [ ] What does God have to say about this in the Word?

- [ ] Is this going to interfere with something else He is asking me to do?

- [ ] To the best of my understanding, does God want me to do this? How can I tell?

- [ ] Can I have peace about this as I do it or will there be an uneasiness?

- [ ] Am I having to rationalize or make excuses or exceptions for myself in order to justify doing/not doing this?

- [ ] What do other Spirit-controlled believers say, especially any He has put over me in spiritual authority?

- [ ] Am I feeling fearful about this? (Sure sign of Satan)

- [ ] Is there an attack on God's goodness/provision/ability to handle this? (Satan's here.)

- [ ] Am I feeling depressed by this? (Satan's probably here.)

- [ ] Am I feeling inadequate in a negative way? (Satan is the accuser of the brethren.)

- [ ] Are all my past negative experiences being brought to mind? (Satan uses the past as a weapon against us.)

- [ ] Am I feeling suspicious about someone's motives, character, actions? (This one can go either way, but most likely it is from Satan, especially if your thoughts are accusatory. If, on the other hand, there is more of a sorrow or sadness that the person may be this way, you well may be feeling the grieving of the Holy Spirit over the person's actions.)

☐ Do I have certain desires or feelings about how I would like this to go? (If so, then be certain you are not allowing your own desires to influence the decision so much that you shut down or ignore the voice of the Spirit to you in order to do things your way.)

Action Step IF-10

Give the Lord carte blanche with your time and finances. Many people feel that what they do with their time, particularly their leisure time, is their own business. That is never true for the believer who wants to walk closely with the Lord. All our time belongs to Him. Those who walk in intimate fellowship do not have time for themselves that cannot be touched. They are always open to the Lord's divine interruptions in their schedules.

The same thing is true of our finances. God is the source of all our income. Therefore, He has the right to ask us to use money we may want to spend in one area for something else. What you will find in such instances is that He will meet your original need in some other, usually unforeseen, way. It is part of our faith-trust walk with Him.

Dian remembers when she first learned this lesson. She raised her own support with Campus Crusade for Christ, and was in the Portland area visiting two of her supporters, Lois, and Mary who is a CPA. It was a cold day just before Thanksgiving, so Dian wore her coat. As she shared her need for $1,500 with Mary, Dian prayed that Mary might be able to help with one or two hundred dollars of the amount. Dian enjoyed the afternoon and evening with her friends and then went home. A couple of days later, as she and her family went out to dinner, she put on her coat for the first time since being with Mary. Much to her surprise her hand found a check. "I immediately went to the phone and called Mary to thank her. Was I ever surprised when she told me what happened. God had shown Mary that the $1,500 she had earmarked for her April taxes was instead to go to my need.

"I really was blown away by that, but felt a responsibility to pray for her to get the money to pay her taxes, since she didn't know where it was coming from. I checked several times, but no money had come in, even by April 1. I spoke with her after April 15, and she told me the Lord had done a wonderful thing—He had let her boss fail to pay her by December 31 some money owed her. This combined with the $1,500 contribution put her into a lower tax bracket, so she didn't have to pay *any* taxes. By doing what God had shown her He wanted her to do, Mary got to have her cake and eat it too. In other words, when she acted in faith to God's promptings, she had a choice: Give the money to the government or give it to Him. We were both thrilled at her choice and His obvious faithfulness."

Action Step IF-11

Cultivate a world vision. As part of cultivating a worldview, we suggest you ask God to help you be more aware of what He wants prayed for in areas outside your own sphere of influence. Use the newspaper, radio and TV news and documentary programs, missionary prayer letters, and any other sources He gives you. Ask Him how to pray for each one that burdens your heart. Your prayer might be something like this:

Dear God

Let me see the world and the needs of others. Let me have Your perspective, to feel what You feel, to have my heart broken by what breaks Yours, and to grieve over what grieves You. Use me to pray Your will into each area. Holy Spirit, guide my praying. If You want me to do something about anything You show me, let me know what and I am available.

Amen

Our perspective has changed over the past forty years from a city perspective to a national perspective to global perspective. Today we have worldwide travel, budgets in billions and a deficit to match, global economy, global threats, and global warming. Things are planned on a larger scale and at a higher cost.

The days when people stood on street corners holding open-air meetings have disappeared. Today we are expected to organize our services well and provide excellence—not that the gospel is ineffective unless it is dressed up. John the Baptist did not have a traveling road show, the best equipment money could buy, or a P. A. system, but he had the same Holy Spirit we have to empower us to share. But think about this: If John the Baptist showed up on *your* corner, clothed in camel's hair and eating locusts and wild honey, would *you* listen to him?

You may realize that you are God's servant in the very best sense of the word. You are a servant because He often asks you to do things for Him that help others and further His kingdom. Such things can be in the physical world in actions, encouragement of others, witnessing, helping, and the like. He will undoubtedly give you many things to pray for that go far beyond your own family interest or even your own sphere of influence or immediate world. Such works are a natural outflow of an intimate walk. You want to help your Friend and Companion in the things that are on His heart and need to be done.

Is this not what best friends do? They care about what is on the heart of their friend; they hurt when their friend hurts; they often take up the offense of their friend. It is very natural that the closer we draw to the Lord, the more our heart is touched with what He cares about, and we put our own concerns on the back burner to meet the needs He desires to be met.

GOD's HIGH STANDARDS

But not only do we care about what concerns our friends, we care about how they think about us. When it is God we are walking with, His standards are high for His companions. But He has given us the ability to meet those standards.

Ephesians 4:1–3 sets out what God wants our lives to be: "Live a life worthy of the calling you have received. Be completely humble and gentle; be patient, bearing with one another in love. Make every effort to keep the unity of the Spirit through the bond of peace." In Romans 12:1–2, he shows us how to do this: "Therefore, I urge you, brothers, in view of God's mercy, to offer your bodies as living sacrifices, holy and pleasing to God—which is your spiritual worship. Do not conform any longer to the pattern of this world, but be transformed by the renewing of your mind. Then you will be able to test and approve what God's will is—his good, pleasing and perfect will."

When we follow this pattern, the fruit of the Spirit is a natural outflow (Gal. 5:22–23). In fact, before Paul wrote about the fruit, he gave a key to meeting God's high standards in verses 16 and 17: "So I say, live by the Spirit, and you will not gratify the desires of the sinful nature. For the sinful nature desires what is contrary to the Spirit, and the Spirit what is contrary to the sinful nature. They are in conflict with each other, so that you do not do what you want." After listing the fruit each Christian is to have because the Holy Spirit indwells them, Paul wrote of another key in this process of living a holy life. Verses 24 and 25 explain: "Those who belong to Christ Jesus have crucified the sinful nature with its passions and desires. Since we live by the Spirit, let us keep in step with the Spirit."

But then there is an interesting warning in the next verse: "Let us not become conceited." Why? Because the flesh has the weakness of pride—yes even spiritual pride. And we can become proud of a good thing—our exemplary walk with the Lord. God does not want us to get caught in this trap, which is so easy to fall into. Paul emphasized this even more just three verses later in Galatians 6:3: "If anyone thinks he is something when he is nothing, he deceives himself."

Pride. What a subtle yet dangerous thing it is in the life of the one desiring to draw closer to God! "Pride goes before destruction" (Prov. 16:18). There are seven things God hates and one of them is pride.[2] The Book of Proverbs is full of warnings against pride. Why? Because pride says, "Look at me. Look at what I am, what I do, what I don't do." Pride compares itself with others.

In God's economy, only He is to be glorified, the one to whom attention is called. Is it not He who gives us the power to live this good Christian life? All we have done is, in essence, to step back and let Jesus live His life in and through us as we draw on the power of the Holy Spirit. We who draw closer to God get to be more like Jesus and less like our old selves. He brings out His best in us.

ENEMY STRATEGIES

The enemy of our souls knows this process all too well,—and where it will end and how negatively his plans will be impacted by a believer who is becoming like Jesus. We can just imagine the consternation in hell as he gets the reports back.

Messenger 1: "Sir, I have terrible news. Remember when we thought we took care of Jesus on the cross? Well, I've just been on the earth, and I am seeing a horrible thing happening in the lives of some of His followers. I had a terrible fright when I looked into the face of the man on Maple Street you sent me to disrupt. I saw glimpses of Jesus in him. What a chilling experience. Please don't send me back again. This man reminds me of when I was in heaven with Jesus, and I just can't stand remembering those days. Have mercy on me."

Messenger 2: "Sir, I had a similar experience in the area where you sent me. I knew it couldn't be, and yet it was. There, in that office building, talking with her boss, was a lady who had so many of the mannerisms of Jesus it was uncanny. I hated being in her presence, but I did succeed in tempting her a little. She thought some words about her boss that *definitely* were "un-Jesus." What a pity, though. She quickly saw what I was doing, and after about five minutes of spewing out those wonderful thoughts, she called them all back as she confessed her sin to God. What an uncomfortable thing to hear. I had to get out of there. It nearly drove me crazy, especially since I thought I had succeeded so well with her."

Messenger 3: "You know, boss, I can't figure out what this world is coming to. We were doing so well; things were improving for us as we got more people to listen to our message and to perform our works. The world was going to hell so nicely. And now look at it. Despite all our major successes recently, there are beginning to be some major cracks in our schemes. Some of these Christians are no longer listening to us like before. It really bugs me. Here I work for years on a person, and then they read a book, listen to someone on radio or TV, or their goody-two-shoes pastor says something that opens their eyes to all I've been doing down through these years. And *poof*—all my work is undone. You know, it's enough to make someone like me crazy. I'm about to give up. What's the use when all my hard work seems for nothing? My existence is getting to be lousy!"

Satan: "Hey, guys! I hear you. I feel your pain. Your pain is my pain. Relax. As always, it takes me and my brains to solve your ineptness. I've found the way to overcome this terrible phenomenon of 'becoming more like Jesus.'

"There are always going to be those pain-in-the-neck people who will not fall for our standard lines. They want to draw closer to our Enemy. But I've been quite successful in getting a number of them to look at how well they are doing. I fight fire with fire. If they want to live a—excuse my language—'holy life,' then let them. I just get them to become proud of their accomplishments, their lack of sin, their good works, their clean life. I point out others who are not doing as well as they are. I drop in those thoughts of, 'How can that person not love the Lord enough to live a better life? Look, if I can do it, anyone can. It's not that hard. It just takes a desire to live right and love the Lord. God is worthy of such a response from us. That person is really bringing shame on the name of the Lord. Maybe I'd better show him how to clean up his act and live right.' Good. Huh? So diabolically subtle, but, oh, so effective. Gets most of them every time. Hey, gang. Try it. You'll like it.

"Remember. You're looking at the few who are like Jesus. Try my method. And forget the small losses. Just keep concentrating on the masses. They are the ones we can manipulate, can pull down, and hopefully get to influence others to think our way, too. Stick to your guns. Use the weapons I've so cleverly given you. After all, am I not the master at deception? The great tempter? These are mere humans. We are much stronger than they. We will win—we have to win—even though our Enemy says we are already defeated.

"We can drop thoughts into these good Christian minds and they will not resist. They will think they thought those thoughts. And don't forget, those who recognize that the thought is wrong and resist it, you simply make them feel guilty 'for being such a wicked person as to think such a thought.' It's a win-win situation. That is, unless they know about this part of my strategy, too. But so few do. Let's keep it that way! Now, out with you all. Go back and make me proud of you. Forward! Tempt! Deceive! Lie! Accuse! Discourage!"

Yes, our enemy tries to tempt us even when we do not fall for his normal line. As we can see from this imaginary conversation, Satan loves to work on our pride. He can trip us up in so many ways; he can broadside us when we are not looking. Is it any wonder Peter warned us about how Satan roams about as a roaring lion seeking whom he can devour? (1 Pet. 5:8) Peter should know; He was told by Jesus that Satan was using him to say what Satan wanted said to Jesus.[3]

Paul was not exempt from this problem, either. He said in Romans 7:15, "I do not understand what I do. For what I want to do I do not do, but what I hate I do." There are some that believe that Paul was not refering to some major evil in his life, but rather that he had become so sensitive to the Spirit of God that doing even the slightest wrong thing caused him great distress and concern. Whether this interpretation is true, it is true that as we draw closer to the Lord—and certainly by this last level—we should not want to do *anything* which would in the *slightest* way offend the Lord.

Our experience is that, first of all, we do not want to do anything even close to wrong. Second, when we do, we are under such conviction that we want to confess it as soon as possible and once again get in a right relationship with God. We immediately sense the grieving of the Holy Spirit and feel ashamed and defiled. It is a painful experience. In some ways it can help us understand the cry from the cross as Jesus became sin and the Father had to turn away from Him: "My God, my God, why have you forsaken me?" (Matt. 27:46). God has not forsaken us, but there is a barrier between us and the Lord which is perceived immediately.

So let us look one final time at the ongoing heart response we will have in some of these major areas we have been tracing.

A CONTINUING HEART PROFILE

This level will never end. You will hopefully walk straight into heaven as an intimate friend of God's.

Reasons for Obedience

Your *obedience* will be *based on* a deep desire to please the Lord. Nothing will be withheld from Him. He will have a right to examine every area of your life. You will not feel nervous or uptight about His desires for you, because you have come to trust Him in your deepest, most inward parts and with the dearest and most treasured things you have.

Degree of Closeness

You will be so *close to God,* you will be inseparable. As we have just described in the section above, you will never want to leave each other's presence. You will do everything you can to stay in the closest of relationships. There will be that constant flow of input between you throughout the day. You will bring the Lord into everything you do.

When you are alone, you may well find yourself talking out loud to Him. In fact, this may have happened several levels earlier. You will feel much of the same type of closeness as you do to your spouse, but even closer since your "Partner" is perfect, will never put you down, and understands you perfectly.

Your Heart's Response

Your *heart's response* will be one of praise, worship, and expressions of love which will flow all the time from you. You will express your love to Him and He, in turn, will tell of His great love for you communicated through the Word, your thoughts, from something you hear on radio, TV, from the pulpit, a friend, or other sources.

As you read the Bible you will find yourself getting new insights or sensing the Lord saying, "This is true for you" as you see a psalm or proverb or other passage that speaks directly to your current circumstance. For Dian one of those times was reading a passage we have already touched on: "Yet the LORD longs to be gracious to you; he rises to show you compassion" (Isa. 30:18). Meditate on this one for a while, and see how your heart responds!

In times of trouble you will find this constant flow between friends intensifies. Your soul will cling more closely to the Lord, and your faith will be a strong shield against the enemy. Often the Lord will give you specific Scriptures to reinforce your faith and to use as a weapon to stop fiery darts of the wicked one. He will remind you of how He has helped in the past and that He is "the same yesterday and today and forever" (Heb. 13:8).

You will have an overwhelming awe at your relationship and how sweet it is. Many days you may find yourself caught up in a sense of a sweeping joy that comes as you worship the Lord and get a fresh or new insight into His majesty, His goodness, and His great care and love for you. Some may find themselves kneeling in adoration; others even lie prone on the floor in holy reverence and rapture of the One who is their Intimate Friend.

Your life will be lived to please the Lord. His desires will be placed above your own. This will include a joyous and absolute surrender to every wish of God. Until this level, you may well have reserved the right to choose whether or not to obey the Lord. But now you are so committed to Him, so in love, so full of faith in Him and His goodness, that you do not hesitate to do what He says.

By now you have given up the right to walk by sight. You do not have to *see* how each detail will work out. You only have to know that because He asks you to do this particular thing, He will cover all bases as you obey and make it come out according to His perfect plan which you can trust.

In essence, there is no struggle in submission. You do what He says when, where, and how He says without having to know every detail ahead of time—sometimes without knowing any details.

Faith and trust are absolute. Your history with the Lord and your study of the Word and application of its truths to your life will have your faith solidly anchored to the Lord. This in turn will give you the ability to trust Him in whatever circumstances come, in all He asks you to do. You believe the best about Him and do not listen to the lies of the enemy in trying to undermine your confidence in God.

Main Focus of Prayer

Your *main focus of prayer and relationship with God* will be one of a continual flow throughout the day, speaking to Him almost as though He were visible beside you, consulting Him about many details of the day, of your future, worshiping Him at times just for who He is. You will pray less for yourself and more for what is on the heart of God. *Your close walk will give you an ever deepening understanding of the Father's heart and what He wants done. You will take up those same desires and pray them back to Him.*[4]

You will find yourself rarely praying anything outside God's will, since you sense what God wants and thus pray these concerns back to Him. You will often find you start thinking about praying for something, and then stop because the Holy

Spirit checks your own spirit that this is not what He wants you to pray. It is definitely one of those "still small voice" situations.

Your life will continue to be fine-tuned since it will always be in progress. His aim is to make you more like Jesus.

Effect of Your Relationship with God on Others

The *effect of your relationship with God on your actions with others* is immense. Those who knew you before you became a believer, or before you began drawing closer to Jesus, should notice a lot of difference. There should be more control of the Spirit and His fruit flowing through you. For example, you should have a strong desire to live at peace with everyone.

Because of your close walk with the Lord and the Word you have learned, you will be *seen by others as a person of great wisdom and self-control.* People will often seek your advice, and you will feel comfortable giving it, knowing that you are speaking truth.

Outlook on Life

Your *outlook on life* will be very positive, very godly. You will have a strong faith which will cause you to be very optimistic and have a deep trust in God's absolute control of all things.

Negative circumstances will have less ability to get you off balance because you are focused on the Lord, have your faith anchored to Him and not the circumstance, and are willing to face the future without fear because you know your God. He is your Intimate Friend. He wants only the best for you and will not lead you down a blind alley or into a trap or dead end. Nor will He desert you or leave you helpless. He will always be beside you, to guide, to smooth out the path, and to make everything work together for good. He is worthy of your trust. You have gotten to know Him intimately.

FINAL THOUGHTS

What a package God has provided for those of us who choose to walk in intimacy with the Lord! Our experience of peace of mind, confidence and security, the joy of relationship, the perfect guidance, and all the other multiplied blessings can not be compared to anything else. It is almost beyond our ability to put into words. Those who walk at this level may well be said to be "living in seventh heaven."

We have been praying for you, that these six chapters on drawing closer to the Lord have been used by Him to help you do just that. We hope you agree that there is nothing greater in life than to experience an intimate relationship with the Lord. In fact, if you do not, you may want to evaluate what is better and be certain that this is not something you are putting between yourself and the Lord.

As we noted in the beginning of our journey, the main key to this whole process, a strategic part of the puzzle, is getting to know our wonderful, awesome God. The better we know Him, the more we can have faith and trust in Him.

Without trust our relationship will wither and be impaired. With it, like the tree planted by the rivers of waters described in Psalm 1, our relationship with the Lord will flourish as our roots go deep into the soil of His Word to take in all the nourishment that is needed to maintain a healthy spiritual life. As we continue to develop our relationship with Jesus—the Living Water—we maintain a healthy, growing life which has the fruit of the Holy Spirit and the lush leaves indicative of God's blessings.

Hebrews 12:2 reminds us that Jesus is the author and finisher of our faith. The more we become like Him, therefore, the stronger our faith will be. Deepen your trust in Him. Let Him "finish your faith." Be aware of anything that would try to come between you or try to make you question the Lord. Guard your faith. Keep it strong. Don't let the enemy get the slightest toehold. Remember, a toehold can become a foothold which develops into a stronghold. Keep every thought under the control of Jesus, and you will successfully resist the sidetracks of the enemy. You will be able to maintain your intimate walk with all the accompanying blessings.

One final thought: Fasting is something the Lord has offered us as a way of slowing down. When combined with prayer, it seems to provide a source of extra power we might not otherwise have to face the problems before us. Jesus indicated this, too.[5] Space does not allow us to go into detail on this, but several good books on the market can help you understand its importance and the various forms of fasting one can do. See the bibliography in resource 3.

Nevertheless, days may come when you will find an imperceptible cooling off, and you may not even know why. We all go through such times. Unfortunately, for some this can cause them to draw back from intimacy and go back even as far as the second level. In the spiritual plane, what is not progressing is usually regressing. In the next chapter we help you know what to do when dry times come. Be prepared. Know what the symptoms are, as well as the causes. In so doing you may avoid unnecessary loss of your first love. May God and you be the most intimate of friends until the return of Jesus Christ or your homegoing!

1. Matthew 5:3,5.

2. Proverbs 6:16–19, KJV.

3. Matthew 16:23.

4. See Ezekiel 22:30 where God desires not to destroy the land. He looks for someone to pray and ask for mercy so He will not have to bring the judgment on the land which otherwise must come.

5. Mark 9:29.

PART THREE

Guarding the Relationship

Chapter 9

What to Do
in the Dry Times

*T*he devil decided to have a garage sale. On the day of the sale, his tools were placed on display for public inspection, each being marked with its sale price. There were a treacherous lot of implements: hatred, envy, jealousy, deceit, lust, lying, pride, and so on.

Set apart from the rest was a harmless-looking tool. It was quite worn and yet priced very high.

"What is the name of this tool?" asked one of the customers, pointing to it.

"That is discouragement," Satan replied.

"Why have you priced it so high?"

"Because it is more useful to me than the others. With that tool, I can pry open a man's heart and get inside—even when I cannot get near him with the other tools. It is badly worn because I use it on almost everyone, since so few people know it belongs to me."

The devil's price for discouragement was high because it is still his favorite tool, and he is still using it on God's people.

Would you not agree that there will be some discouraging times in life? Times when things just don't seem to go as planned? You get on the freeway, heading off to work. You thought you had given yourself plenty of time, only to find that the car right in front of yours has broken down. Or how about that raise you thought you deserved? And why are the kids not doing as well in school as you had hoped for? Satan has certainly fine-tuned his attacks with disappointment. We can be disappointed by people, places, and things. And more often than not, we find that the end result will be a spiritually dry time.

If we are going to make it in life we must learn how to deal with disappointment. In our Bibles there is a man who was an authority when it came to dealing with the disappointment caused by people. And by examining the life of Moses we can learn three important truths about dealing with the disappointment we will all face.

First, we must remember that mountaintop experiences in life often have valleys on both sides. No one has ever put up with more complaining than a leader by the name of Moses. Complaining was the favorite pastime of the Israelites. Complaining was the sin that kept them out of the promised land.

Their philosophy was, "When in doubt, criticize." They were very quick to criticize their leaders. One particular time the Israelites were having trouble with water; they were always having trouble with water. First, there was too much water at the Red Sea; then not enough water while they were in the desert: "Then Moses led Israel from the Red Sea and they went into the Desert of Shur. For three days they traveled in the desert without finding water. When they came to Marah, they could not drink its water because it was bitter. (That is why the place is called Marah.)" (Ex. 15:22–23). This was no small problem:

three million thirsty people and lots of thirsty animals and there is no water in the desert.

But notice the words "For three days . . . ." What had happened *three* days ago? They had crossed the Red Sea, that is what had happened. This had been a great spiritual victory. But mountaintop experiences so often precede a trip into a valley, and this is precisely what happened to the people of Israel.

The people were probably wondering, "What went wrong?" But look at verse 25. "Then Moses cried out to the LORD, and the LORD showed him a piece of wood. He threw it into the water, and the water became sweet. There the LORD made a decree and a law for them, *and there he tested them*" (emphasis added).

After almost a combined half-century of ministry both authors soon learned that our character and our faith is revealed not in the big crises of life, but in the small crises of life. As Christians we are a lot like tea bags. We really do not know what's on the inside, until we are in hot water. God may have showed His might and His power when He parted the Red Sea, but when the people of Israel came to Marah, the true character of the Israelites was revealed. God led them there to test them.

Have you been going through a test recently? Dry times and disappointments are tests. They test what we are really like on the inside. Notice that the Red Sea events are not described like this. And the Israelites, because of their complaining, failed the test. So what is your "Marah" today? Your Marah is anything that is distasteful to you. It is what was once sweet, but now has become bitter. It can be your job, a relationship, a problem. Realize that whatever it is, it is probably the result of the natural flow of mountaintop and valley experiences.

Second, serving people can create dry times because of their forgetfulness. Let's examine Exodus 15:24: "So the people grumbled against Moses, saying, 'What are we to drink?'" The people of Israel had a short memory; just three days earlier, the Red Sea was parted. We do the same thing to others and even to God, "What have you done for me lately?" We forget all about what God has done in the past. We forget how many times God has rescued us and guided us in the past. It is so sad how human nature works and so easily forgets.

Children forget their parents; bosses forget the contributions of workers; spouses take their mates for granted. We will do great service for people, and guess what, they will forget it.

So discouragement can come, a cooling off, a lukewarmness can set into our relationship with the Lord. But God is the Master Psychologist. He knows exactly what makes us tick, what will give us back the spark we have lost in our relationship with Him. This is one reason He had the children of Israel remember the things He had done for them. They needed the reminders of His faithfulness. They couldn't just depend on their memory.

Action Step DT-1

Make a personalized "What to Do in Dry Times" list. In it list different things that have been meaningful to you, especially in good times. This could include the following:

- Verses. Write them out so you do not later have to look them up.

- Songs, especially worship and praise. Writing out the words of a favorite song that touches your heart can be meaningful when you are down and be something the Lord can use to lift your spirits. Dwell on those words that have spoken so clearly in the past of His goodness and faithfulness.

- Statements, poems, thoughts, or anything else that has touched your heart and helped you draw closer to the Lord at some point.

- Prayers you or others have written, expressing your love, joy, faith, trust, and confidence in the Lord.

- Special things God has done for you and/or ways you have seen Him work in your life.

- Important answers to prayers.

- During the good times, write yourself a letter about the reasons it is good. Tell yourself how great it is, what you feel, why, what is most important to you, where your focus is, and any other thing that you see as a part of this experience. David did this often. He wrote himself a psalm exhorting his soul in effect to shape up and trust in the Lord: "You will still see His goodness" (Ps. 42:5).

- When you are in a dry time, review all of the above plus the other material you have in your journal, such as the attributes and emotions pages. These will help to refocus you on the Lord and remind you of His greatness and faithfulness.

Also in the next three sections, be certain to add anything that is specific to you that we have not listed.

Action Step DT-2

Ask the Lord to show you why you have gotten "dry." Put a mark by any statement you can say "yes" to.

- ☐ Are your eyes on people or circumstances, not the Lord?

- ☐ Are you getting self-centered more than God-centered?

- ☐ Are you feeling unfulfilled or that your expectations/needs are not being met? Have you let your prayer times slip or become routine?

- ☐ Is there unconfessed sin? Something you are resisting that the Lord has shown you to do/not to do?

- ☐ Have you let something get between you and the Lord? A family member or friend, work, ministry, a project or "good work," possession?

- ☐ Has pride in your relationship with the Lord gotten you off track?

- ☐ Have you judged others, feeling they were less spiritual?

- ☐ Are you judging your relationship by your feelings and not by what is truth?

Now, on a piece of paper, write down your answer to each question you have marked.

- Why you think you have allowed this problem to occur.
- What started the problem?
- What caused it to increase?
- What should you do in order to correct the problem?
- What may keep you from doing so?
- What Scriptures are appropriate to claim to help get you back into God's perspective on this? See the next section for help. Also a *Nave's Topical Bible* and a *Strong's* or *Young's Concordance* will help find verses in a given subject area. You may also want to consult the bibliography for more ideas of books to read.

Action Step DT-3

A good tool to help you evaluate what has happened is to go back to the original eighty-eight question test in chapter 2. Retake the test. You will probably find that questions you could once answer yes have now become no's. Ask the Lord to show you why this is true.

In this next section we will be looking at principles we violate that can lead to trouble. Try to identify any principles you are violating. Ask the Lord to show you how to stop them and bring them under the control of Jesus (2 Cor. 10:3–5). The following may help you identify some. In no way is this an exhaustive list. The enemy will give you negative thoughts that will fit your own personality, weaknesses, and situation. So be sensitive to your "self-talk"—those negative things you are always saying to yourself that, were they said by anyone else, would cause you to feel hurt or even depressed. "You're such a slob!" "I'm always messing up." Sometimes we are our own worst critic, often because we listen to the accuser of the brethren as he tells us things about ourselves in order to make us ineffective.

WHAT HAPPENS WHEN WE LISTEN TO SATAN'S LIES

The enemy of our souls wants to do everything he can to knock us out of the race, to sidetrack us, discourage us. In the next chapter we will look at this in more detail. Here are nine principles we have identified that believers often violate in evaluating their relationship with the Lord and in implementing the drawing closer process.

A. Satan will always try to undermine our confidence in God. If he can get us to mistrust God by our having a wrong view of Him, then he will dilute the effectiveness of our efforts to draw closer. In fact, he may well sidetrack us. You cannot have a close relationship with someone you fear or do not trust.

B. One of the reasons we can get into dry times is because we get our eyes off the Lord and onto circumstances—the very circumstances He has allowed into our lives to draw us closer to Him. We start walking by sight.

C. Our feelings and emotions can cause us to reject truth if we put more faith in how we feel than in what God says. Relying on our feelings as the authority for any situation in our lives is to put them above God as our guide.

D. Because of humanity's fallen condition, we all have weaknesses, including a poor self-image. Therefore, we are vulnerable to attacks on our self-image. Satan wants us to feel unworthy, incapable, disqualified. He does this in relation to our interaction with others and with God.

E. Putting our needs and desires before God will always create problems. There will be a constant pull between the two. We may get our way but lose the battle and in turn the blessings that come from putting God's will first in our life.

F. Laziness. The second law of thermodynamics—which talks about everything running down—seems to come into play. In this fast-paced culture of today, humans get bored easily; they want variety and change, they think they need constant stimulation in order to feel satisfied. These are not the best elements to developing a lasting relationship. Time, effort, and persistence are needed. Is this not why there are so few world-class athletes? Why so many marriages are breaking up? Satan will work on this weakness, too.

G. Impatience. Too often we want everything to happen right now. We want instant relationship, instant closeness. When we do not see things developing as quickly as we want, then we may get impatient and want to quit. Satan will try to get you to do just that in the drawing closer process.

H. Rationalization, excuses. We may get caught in the trap of giving excuses for why we are an exception to something we see in the Word, or why we are not doing what we know the Lord wants. We try to come up with excuses that will pacify our conscience, that will satisfy God so the Holy Spirit will no longer convict us. This has been an area Satan has used successfully since Adam and Eve.

I. Wrong Motives. God has promised so much to us. But sometimes the enemy of our souls will try to twist the good things God has promised and make us try to earn them through our good works. Another version of this deception is to make us think that as long as we are doing all God is asking us to do, then we will have a "bed of roses" in our life, or that God owes us something—a new car, a spouse, a better job. "If I do _____, then God will have to _____ ."

Action Step DT-3

What negative thoughts are running through your mind about you, your relationship with God, and the process of drawing closer? Mark any of the following that you recognize are true of you. Then, where appropriate, write what the truth is. You will see one or more letters—A, B, C, D, E, F, G, H, I—behind each statement. These letters refer to the section above, which lists the principles we can violate. With each marked statement, go before the Lord, confess the wrong thinking, and tell Him what is truth. Then ask the Holy Spirit to help you stop thinking this way, to reprogram your mind, and to bring every thought under the control of Jesus as commanded in 2 Corinthians 10:3–5. Ask Him to help you determine what you need to do to reverse this lie and its effects in your life.

☐ My quiet time is boring. Why be a hypocrite and continue on? (C, E, F)

☐ This is not meeting my needs. It is a waste of time. (C, E, F)

☐ You are not really a "friend of God." He only helps you because you are His child and He has to. But He doesn't *like* you. (A, D)

☐ There is nothing special about you. Why should God care about you? (A, D)

☐ I'm not sure I'm getting anywhere with this Bible study. I don't understand all of it. I might as well give it up. (C, G)

☐ I pray all day long, so I don't have to have a special time with God. My whole day is special with Him. (F, G)

☐ I'm so busy right now. I don't have time to have my quiet time. But God knows my heart and He'll understand. I'll do more later when I'm not so busy. (E, F, H)

☐ I'm not sure God listens when I pray. So why waste my time. (A, C, D, H)

☐ Maybe I'm just fooling myself in thinking God is answering my prayers and wants a close relationship. (A, B, C, D)

☐ Does God understand what I'm going through? Does He care? (A, B, D)

☐ God isn't fair. I've done all this Bible study and prayer, and now *(negative event)* happens. *(A, B, C, I)*

☐ I'm too tired to pray. I'll do it another time. (C, E, F, H)

☐ God knows what I need, so why bother to tell Him. (F, H)

☐ I messed up on _____. God will never forgive me for letting Him down. I've blown our relationship. (A, B, C, D)

☐ Drawing closer is just a concept someone wrote. I'm not sure it is working. How do I know it is from God? (B, H)

☐ I don't like some of the things I'm reading in the Bible. They may have been all right for those days, but I'm not sure they are for today. (C, E, H, I)

☐ It seems like I'm always feeling guilty every time I read the Bible. I don't need this added pressure. (C, D, E, H, I)

☐ There are just too many rules and regulations to follow. I'll never be able to live up to them all. So why try anymore. (A, C, D, E, F, G, H, I)

☐ I don't feel like quiet time. I'll do it later. (C, E, F, H)

☐ When I'm sick like this, it's too hard to have a quiet time. (C, E, F, H)

☐ As I've gotten older my (sickness, ailment) keeps me from feeling like spending very much time with the Lord. I'm sure He understands. (B, C, E, F, H)

☐ My brain doesn't function as it used to. I don't think I can keep my Bible reading and in-depth praying up any more. (B, C, D, E, F, H)

☐ If God really loved me, He wouldn't have let happen. I'm not sure I like or can trust Him any more. (A, B, C, E, I)

☐ This problem is so great that I can't concentrate on my time with the Lord. (B, C, E, H)

☐ My grief is so great that I can't really communicate with God. I'm overwhelmed. (B, C, E, H)

☐ I'm not sensing God as I used to. Maybe this isn't going to work, and I should just give up. (A, B, C, D, G, H)

☐ I thought I'd feel closer to God than I do if I did this. Maybe this isn't working. (C, G, H, I)

☐ I don't need to spend much special time with the Lord. I've already spent so much with Him until now, that I know all there is to know in our relationship. What more can I learn? (A, C, E, F, H, I)

☐ If God really loves me, why does He let me go through these trials? (A, B, C, D, E, I)

☐ Why does God let me have such a strong temptation? (A, B, C, D, E, G, H, I)

☐ There must be something wrong in my relationship with God, or else I wouldn't have (gotten sick/ had this accident, etc.). (A, B, C, D, I)

☐ If I keep on drawing closer to God, He is going to ask me to do something I don't want to do. (A, C, D, E, H, I)

☐ I feel so lousy about myself right now, how can anyone, even God, like me? (A, B, C, D)

Note: The above questions should also serve as guidelines to help you identify where you are in your "dry period," as discussed in the next section of the four critical points.

But before we move on, let us give you three questions we have found helpful when such thoughts come to mind.

First, is this something I want to be true?

Second, is this something God says is true?

Third, if I do not want to believe this and God does not want me to believe it, then what is the source of this thought? As we used to say in our games of tag, Satan is "it."

FOUR CRITICAL POINTS

In any relationship—whether we are discussing a marriage, siblings, or our relationship with God—we will face periods of frustration and stagnation. In fact, we have identified four critical points which may need addressing in the life of all believers who desire their relationship with the Lord Jesus to grow deeper and closer. These four critical points are illustrated in the following diagram, to which we will often refer in our explanation.

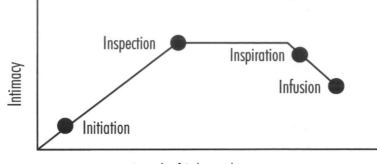

Length of Relationship

Note: It may be wise to follow all instructions for any dry area level you have already passed. For example, if you are at inspiration, you should look at the corrective material for Initiation and Inspection and do those that are appropriate for your situation.

Recognize that at any level, it may take some effort to get back on track since you have let yourself drift into this dry area and have not resisted it. Thought patterns, habits, and other tools the enemy has used against you may not be easy to give up unless you are ready to totally surrender to the control of the Spirit. We therefore recommend you review "How to Be Filled with the Spirit" in chapter 4.

Initiation

The first critical point, initiation, refers to the time directly after conversion when a person desires to deepen their walk with Jesus but does not know how. Such people may go to church but not understand. They could be in a group of other believers who get together for encouragement and growth, and yet be afraid to ask questions for clarification. They try to read their Bible, but they become overwhelmed with terminology and content. A dry time, even in the beginning, may be the result.

To grow beyond the dry times of initiation, a person must do three things as we send out an *S.O.S.* for help.

Seek the Lord. We need to pray, read the Bible, and listen to Him. Ask the Lord to restore your first love for Him. Allow Him to woo you through the Word and through His loving care for you. Go back to Action step DT-1 and choose some or all of those things to.

Obey Him. As you listen to the Lord, He will show you things He wants you to know and to do. If there is unconfessed sin that has blocked the free flow of your fellowship or your feelings, confront it, trusting Him that whatever has been the source of the sin has not been worth the great loss you have encountered. You will be much better off dealing with it quickly. Recognize that He loves you so much and wants the best for you. Whatever He shows you will be the right thing. Therefore, trust Him and obey what He shows—and keep on obeying Him. Have patience in this turnaround for everything may not come in your timing. It is usually a process.

Stay focused. Stay focused on the goal of relationship and growth while paying attention to the voice of the Lord and to what other Spirit-led believers say. At the same time learn to recognize and therefore resist what the enemy says. Do not let your eyes get focused on your feelings and emotions as much as on the Lord. He alone and what He says should be your guideline for what is true. Walk by faith, not by sight. When doubts start to come after you have prayed, you can say, "Thank You, Lord, that You are in the process of restoring my spiritual strength and desire."

Inspection

The second critical point in the growth of a Christian which could produce a dry time is that of inspection. This could come after a month, a year, or a decade in the life of a Christian, because this critical point represents that time when you are convinced that you have learned most of what is available in Christian circles and begin to plateau in your walk with God. You may have all the principles in place in your life—a regular quiet time, an adequate prayer life and even regular service within a local church family—yet you begin to sense that something is missing and you have no idea how to fill this void.

This critical point is not unusual in the life of most followers of Jesus Christ. You might remember from our discussion of level 5, Good Friend, that there will be times in your search to draw closer to God that will be more difficult than others.

Some people with a "religious" upbringing have great difficulty seeing God Almighty as a Good Friend, because their background prohibited intimacy with the God of the universe. When you shut down a natural forward movement of a relationship, inevitably problems will arise. As we have mentioned, something floating in the ocean is either going forward or backwards in relation to the shore. So if you are not careful to keep moving forward, a dry plateau in your life will be the result.

What do you need to do if you find yourself heading for this negative situation or if you have already become comfortable maintaining this plateau in your relationship? Let us share five things which you can do to bring a *S.P.A.R.K.* back to your search to draw closer.

Search your heart and motives. There will be one or more things that will have contributed to this backward movement in your relationship. As you have been reading this chapter, it is quite likely the Lord has already shown you part or all of your problem. You need to confess it and get rid of the negative results it has produced in blocking your fellowship with the Lord.

Pray with variety. Variety is the spice of life, and is also desirable in our prayers. In our book *Power House*[1] the resource section is full of ideas on different kinds of prayer. Resource 2 has a great fourteen-day experiment designed especially to give a wide variety of prayer experiences.

Ask for help. There are many great devotionals (see resource 3). In addition, you can ask friends for their help by finding out what works for them. Especially note the first action step in this chapter. Many ministries have excellent tapes available. See a listing of them in resource 4 of *Power House.*[2] Rereading some or all of this book may help to identify things you have allowed to creep in that have caused you to drift.

Read the Scriptures. Read fresh areas that you have not been in before, but at the same time don't neglect Psalms and Proverbs for regular input that will uplift and encourage your heart and help you gain godly wisdom. Keep your pen and journal pages handy.

Know your enemy's strategy. Paul warned us to be aware of the enemy's schemes.[3] You need to do the same in order to avoid any traps, detours, ambushes, or anything else he may try to use to sideline you or at least diminish the effectiveness of your Christian walk and your closeness with the Lord. Along with some of the materials in this chapter, especially action steps DT-2,3. Remind yourself that you are not the first person to have these problems. Many have gone through just what you are and have come out on the other side successfully. They simply had to apply God's principles to do it.

Inspiration

The third critical point is inspiration and reflects the time in a believer's life when he or she failed to recognize a period of plateau—which we have called inspection—and began a slow downhill slide away from God. This level may be demonstrated in sporadic church attendance, a failure to read the Bible and pray, a loss of desire to associate with other believers, a slight degradation of moral decisions, and an obvious change in spiritual language and motivation to please God.

This is the natural consequence of an extended plateau because growth has ceased and a person's sphere of influence has changed. If they are unable to restructure their lives and recatch the vision and what John called "first love," they soon find themselves on a slippery slope away from God, His morals, His ethics, and His will for their lives. Needless to say, they have embarked on a very dry time.

What are their needs? If you find yourself at critical point three, you can take specific steps to rekindle the passion before the hardening of your heart begins to take place.[4] The key is the restoration of *H.O.P.E.*

Have a time of evaluation. Work through all the above action steps. Ask the Lord to show you which areas are true for your situation. Ask Him to show you other specific things that may not be listed. Deal with any unconfessed sin. This is critical to the restoration of your hope. Guilt will always destroy hope.

Open the Word. The Word will be very important to reestablishing a firm foundation for your walk and in undoing wrong thinking. We suggest you read Psalms, Proverbs, Philippians, and Ephesians. Write down what the Lord shows you and then do it.

Pray for insight. Talking in a meaningful way will be an important part of restoring hope. You may want to pray similar to the following:

> *Lord,*
> *I have been drifting from You and it hurts. I want to be close; I want to feel what I used to. I've really lost my first love for You without knowing how. Please help me in finding my way back to that close relationship I had with You. Show me what lies of the enemy I've believed, what weaknesses of the flesh I've allowed to influence me, what wrong thinking I've had. Give me Your perspective, Your solution. I need a fresh vision and renewed hope. Show me how You see me and Your love for me. Thank You for not giving up on me! Help me to strip away all that has become a barrier in our relationship. Help me to want to do Your will.*

Enjoy the Lord again. When you unblock a drain, you can expect the water to flow again. In the same way, when we remove the things that we've allowed to block our fellowship with the Lord and to shut down our emotions, we can expect to once again be able to enjoy Him as we have before. But remember, you've been on a side track. It may or may not take time to get back to where you were. But know that it will come. Expect there to be a growing new dimension in your walk with the Lord. Repeat to Him your words of love, faith, confidence, and other statements that will renew your own emotions and tell your feelings how they are to respond. Remember the good times you've had with the Lord.

Infusion

Our society does not accept delayed gratification very well. We want hope—now! We want growth—now! And we want patience—now! What happens to many is they become disillusioned by the timing and/or circumstances of their development. Others may find that routine has set in, they have not felt challenged enough, or they are just plain bored. The spiritual warfare that comes in developing a dynamic, vibrant relationship with the Lord has taken its toll. You have spiritual life, but it is not healthy. At this stage you need to take an *E.K.G.* of your faith.

Examine your heart. Paul said to examine your heart to see if you really are in the faith.[5] There can be no relationship without being born again. Many people in churches today who call themselves Christians, in fact have never been born again. They know about God, try to follow His ways, love Him, may even pray to Him, and ask Him to be with them. But they have never asked Him to come into their lives; they have never made that total surrender of their lives to Him. If you feel this may describe you, and you want to be in a right relationship with God, then you will want to read chapter 4 again and take the necessary steps to become a child of God and establish relationship. Without this step, no one can reach heaven. Also examine your heart to see that there is no unconfessed sin. Sin will always interfere in the drawing closer process, shutting it down completely. Deal with each and every thing the Lord shows you.

Keep your hope. When we look at the Lord in the midst of our troubles, our faith is strengthened and our hope encouraged. To look at circumstances is to be devastated, to give up hope, because apart from the Lord there is no hope. After you have asked God's help, believe He will do what you asked, in part because He wants it even more than you do. Then every time you are tempted to doubt or get discouraged because you do not see the progress you'd like, express your faith and confidence in God by saying, "Thank You, Lord, that You are in the process of (name the prayer request)."

Give your life back to the Lord. You have allowed a cooling down of your love for the Lord. Now you want to rekindle the fire. One thing to do is to ask the Lord to once again take control of your life, to give you back your first love, to help you have Him as first in your life. You might want to pray similar to the following or combine this prayer with the one in the above section:

> *Lord*
>
> *I have allowed my love to grow so cold for You, it almost seems as if it is out. But I want so much to have it back, but until now have not known how to do so. Thank You for showing me what has been the problem. Help me to recognize when I am starting to think wrongly and then show me how to keep every thought under Your control.*

DO NOT GIVE UP HOPE

Let us get back to our original story of Moses and the children of Israel. A lot of complaining had taken place and the people were not happy. The first thing Moses did was to give this dry time to God. He let it go. *"Then Moses cried out to the* LORD *and the* LORD *showed him a piece of wood. He threw it into the water, and the water became sweet. There the* LORD *made a* decree and a law for them, and there he tested them" (Ex. 15:25, emphasis added).

The first thing that Moses did was not to write a letter to the editor and get upset; he did not start a chain of gossip in the office to discuss how someone had mistreated him; he did not even try to build a case for himself; he took it right to the Lord. The first thing we need to do when we face a dry time is—pray. Now, think about your "Marah" for a moment. What is the bitter thing in your life right now? It could be a physical Marah, an emotional Marah, a vocational Marah; it is just something that has not turned out the way you hoped it would. And when you are able to turn this dryness over to God, He alone has the resources and ability to change the condition and/or the circumstances.

Thinking about disappointment and dry times—if there was anyone in the Bible that had a right to be disappointed, it was Joseph. He had a dream as a young man, that his family would one day bow down to him. But his brothers did not like the dream and eventually sold Joseph into slavery. In slavery, he was falsely accused of rape and put in jail.

The first forty years of Joseph's life was one giant downhill slide, past what we may have considered all the critical points previously discussed. He had every right to be upset, to say, "Lord, this isn't fair. I don't like what's going on." But later in his life when Joseph was in a position of prominence, his brothers came to him asking for help. He had the perfect chance to get even, but he did not. And in one of the great passages in the Bible, Joseph shares, "You intended to harm me, but God intended it for good to accomplish what is now being done, the saving of many lives" (Gen. 50:20).

One of the most popular words in our society today is the word *victim*. And the fact is that there are many experiences in your life that you have no control over. Some have been hurt very deeply by family members, school teachers, friends, parents, or former husbands and wives. But you can choose not to be a victim.

God has the power to help you overcome any and every circumstance. Romans 8:28 clearly states, "And we know that in all things God works for the good of those who love him, who have been called according to his purpose."

That does not say everything *is* good, but everything *works together* for good. If someone gets cancer, that is not good; it is bad. If someone is abused, that is not good; it is bad. The fact is that person may have meant it for bad, but God can use it for good. God works in all things, even the bad stuff. When Marahs, disappointments, come into my life, those experiences I do not like, I do not run from them or try to hide them. I need to pray about it and allow God to work in and through the situation.

In Moses' life, God provided a way to turn the bitter experience into a sweet experience. Exodus 15:25 states, "Then Moses cried out to the LORD, *and the* LORD *showed him a piece of wood.* He threw it into the water, and the water became sweet. There the LORD made a decree and a law for them, and there he tested them" (emphasis added).

Notice that God showed Moses the wood. Circle the word *showed*. It doesn't say God created this wood; He showed him the wood. Do you know why? Because the solution had been there all along, but when we wallow in self-pity we cannot see it. And the answer to your dry time is within sight, when you put your eyes on the Lord and allow Him to direct you. As children of God we can be assured that God will meet our needs and restore the spiritual flames. Look at Exodus 15:27; "Then they came to Elim, where there were twelve springs and seventy palm trees, and they camped there near the water." They were once out of water, and now this shortage is followed by Palm Springs. This area was miles and miles of barren desert, and right in the middle, God provides an oasis. This was paradise.

Question: How far is Elim from Marah? If you were to get out a map, you would discover that they are only about five to ten miles apart. But the people had just stopped too soon. They gave up—too soon.

At the close of the first day of the Battle of Shiloh, with serious Union reverses, General U. S. Grant was met by his greatly discouraged chief engineer, James McPherson, who said: "Things look bad, General. We've lost half our artillery and a third of our infantry. Our line is broken and we are pushed back nearly to the river." Grant made no reply, and McPherson impatiently asked what he intended to do. "Do? Why reform the lines and attack at daybreak. Won't they be surprised!" Surprised they were. The Confederate troops were routed before nine o'clock that morning. No one is defeated until he gives up. So do not quit, the answer may just be five miles away.

Now here is another question: How do you get from Marah to Elim? How do you get from the place of dry time to the place of delight? How can you get from pain to paradise? We have covered several steps in our examination of the critical points of drawing closer, but let us add one more: You just keep on going. This passage does not say that God brought Elim to them; it says that they had to keep going despite their feelings. And it is the same with us. "But I'm tired. I don't feel like serving anymore. I don't feel like praying any more. I don't like tithing or like going to church or like reading the Bible." What do you do when you do not feel like doing those things? You do them.

Can you imagine calling your workplace tomorrow and saying, "Boss, you know, my heart really isn't into going to work today. I don't feel like being there. And I know you wouldn't want me to be a hypocrite. So, since I don't feel like being there, I'm just going to stay home, watch soap operas, and relax."

Most of the great things in life are done by people who did not feel like doing them. That is a mark of maturity. People who solely live by their feelings are immature. God wants us to live by commitments. We may not always feel like being available to our family, but we do, because we are committed to be there for them. To be honest, some days, even ministers find it hard to go to work. People have problems and sometimes the load a person carries in the ministry is almost too much to bear. It does not matter. It is a question of spiritual commitment.

Action Step DT-4

When you have successfully worked your way back to the right path with the Lord and your first love is reestablished, you may find it helpful to write yourself a letter or some notes about what you have learned. Write about what needs to be avoided in the future or telltale signs of impending problems. Also list things that were meaningful or helpful in getting back to the Lord.

Many of us get stuck in our dry times, when we need to go through them, to get out of Marah and go on to Elim. You know, we have not experienced every pain in life, but in our forty-five plus years of ministry, nothing shocks us any more. We have seen such incredible disappointments in some people's lives that most people would have said, "No way can anyone come out of that." But the power of God brings people out of Marah into Elim. Some of you are in Marah right now. That does not mean you missed God's will. But even if you are in a dry place because you missed God's will, it does not matter. In either case, God knows exactly where you are right now—just don't give up. You are His child. He loves you and wants the best for you. Psalm 34:18 promises every one of us, "The LORD is close to the brokenhearted and saves those who are crushed in spirit."

Two thousand years ago, God turned the bitter experience of a cross into the opportunity for a sweet relationship with the Son of God. Jesus Christ bore the sins of humanity upon Himself so that you could be set free, and you could have this peace of mind in the midst of dry times.

◆

1. *Power House*, 109–225.

2. Ibid., 135–143.

3. 2 Corinthians 2:11.

4. Hebrews 3:13.

5. 2 Corinthians 13:5.

The Joy of the Journey

So how have you done in our journey of drawing closer to the Lord and going deeper in your faith? Have you completed your puzzle? If you are reading this, you have not. For no one will complete it until they see Him face to face. But now you should be able to see through that dark glass more clearly,[1] you have a much better understanding of what the end picture will look like. Each day you continue to work on the puzzle, drawing closer to the Lord, you will see more and more of it.

In some ways we are like a person on a journey across the mountains to a distant city. At the point of salvation we reached the mountain peak and have an obscure glimpse of the city very far off in the distance—only a dot on the horizon. But with each day's, week's, month's, year's travel, we get closer to our destination—as long as we stay headed in the right direction.

———

Unfortunately, sometimes we get lured onto side roads, lose our sense of direction, and unintentionally start heading either parallel to our path or actually away from it. The King of the city will see that we reach Him eventually, but we may not enjoy the journey as much as we might have had we stayed on the road He laid out for us to travel. The Companion and Friend He wanted us to walk with may have been forsaken by us too at times, because we chose to turn left when He was leading us right. We didn't lose Him as a Friend, only the privilege of fellowship with Him for a time. He will come looking for us as the Good Shepherd did for the little lost lamb, but hopefully we will not have strayed too far and gotten too wounded in the process.

To a greater degree we decide how easy this journey will be, how delightful. We can choose to be an intimate friend with the Lord and enter heaven walking close to Him, or we can stray off His path and end up with cuts and bruises, disillusionment, and discouragement. We will get there all right, but the choice is ours as to which level of fulfillment it will be.

We know what the Lord's heart is and His desire for us. He expressed it so well in many places. He is compassionate and gracious, slow to anger, abounding in love and faithfulness.[2] He coaxes us, woos us to draw nearer, to have sweet fellowship, to experience the depths of His loving heart. He does not want to rush us, but, oh, how much He longs for an intimate friendship with us: "Come to me, all you who are weary and burdened, and I will give you rest" (Matt. 11:28). He encourages us to draw near to Him and He will draw near to us.[3] He is not pushy. He is there, waiting for us with outstretched arms, but we must make the first move. He softly whispers, "I have loved you with an everlasting love" (Jer. 31:3).

He reassures us, "The LORD your God is with you, he is mighty to save. He will take great delight in you, he will quiet you with his love, he will rejoice over you with singing" (Zeph. 3:17). Allow the Lord to sing over you. Allow Him to rejoice over you and you in Him. Relish the closeness, the warm friendship, the ecstasy of being with your Beloved, feeling fully accepted and wanted, knowing that He delights in you, is satisfied with you, and wants the very best for you. Rejoice in His joy over you. Know that this is just a taste of His love lavished on you for all eternity. Bask in the warmth of this love from the One who is love.[4] Let it go through every pore, removing the hurts of others, of the past.

Walk in complete and secure fellowship with your wonderful Lord. Plumb the depths of His greatness, and let your spirit soar as you behold His might and majesty revealed in creation and unfolded in awesome splendor as you walk together. Marvel at His perfection and wonder at His gentleness, compassion, meekness, and humility. Envelop yourself in all He is. Enjoy a loving relationship that can never be broken, never be in jeopardy. You are accepted unconditionally by the greatest Person in all the universe—its Creator, Sustainer, and King. He is your Savior and at the same time your promised Husband. He is a warm and loving Father. Your heart wants to respond in love and wants to please so loving a Companion, so good and intimate a Friend. You are your Beloved's and He is yours.[5] Walk with Him in the close intimacy of transparent love and acceptance.

Come. "The Spirit and the bride say, 'Come'" (Rev. 22:17).

◆

1. 1 Corinthians 13:12, KJV.
2. Psalm 86:15.
3. James 3:8, NASB.
4. 1 John 4:8.
5. Song of Solomon 2:16.

The Attributes
and Characteristics of God

How to get the most from your study of God:

1. Begin with prayer, asking God to show you truth.

2. Make a separate page for each attribute on loose leaf paper in your notebook.

3. Work through each attribute with paper and pen, noting anything that seems important. Also jot down any questions that may arise. Ask God to show you the answers, but don't let the questions stop you from going on. Later, when He shows you the answer, jot it down along with the date. If you date the question, it will show you how long it took for Him to show you the answer. This will be an encouragement of His faithfulness and His ability to know what you want to know.

4. The verses for each attribute are in sequential order for ease in looking them up. Those we feel are most important are in bold face. You may want to read these first to identify the attribute, then use the others to build on that foundation.

5. New ideas will come to you, later, as you think about what you are learning or through materials you read or hear. Be certain to keep a record of these ideas on the appropriate attribute page.

6. List problems you are facing right now in your life. As you study this material, write down any attribute or characteristic you see that will help you solve your problem.

Questions to ask yourself as you study the attributes and characteristics: (Note: Not all questions may apply to each attribute/characteristic.)

1. How is this perspective of God different from what you have thought about Him in this area? You will find it helpful to write the truth about God as you now understand it, in order to erase any wrong understanding you have previously had.

2. Why is this an important characteristic of God?

3. What if God were not this way?

4. How secure would you be if He were not this way? How would you feel?

5. How important is this truth to your life? How does it make you feel that God is_____?

6. Are there any changes you should make because of this truth? Why? or Why not?

7. Where have you observed this characteristic in nature, in your life, or in others?

LEVEL 1: HOLY SOVEREIGN

"Holiness" expresses the sum total of all God is. "Sovereign" expresses the absolute rulership of God above everything and everyone else. He is under no external constraints. (**Isa. 46:5,9,10**; Zech. 9:14; 1 **Tim. 6:16–17**)

Creator:

The Bible declares God is responsible for the creation of everything that exists anywhere. It also says that He keeps all things running properly (sustains it). (**Ps. 136:5–9**; **Isa. 40:25–26**; **44:24**; **45:12**; Jer. 5:22; 10:12; 51:15,16; Dan. 5:23; **Acts 17:24–26**; Heb. 1:1)

Majesty:

The greatness and dignity of God , His splendor. (Ps. 93:1; 96:6; 104:1; **145:5**; Isa. **2:10,19**; 24:14; Heb. 1:3; 8:1; 2 Peter 1:16)

All-powerful:

The ability to do anything and everything He wishes that is not contrary to His nature. (Gen. 18:14; **Ps. 33:9–11**; 93:4; **Isa. 40:26**; **46:10**; **Jer. 32:17**; **Matt. 19:26**; **Luke 1:37**; **Rom. 1;19,20**; **Rev. 19:6**)

Present everywhere:

God fully fills all places of the universe at all times. (1 **Kings 8:27**; **Ps. 139:3,5,7–12**; Isa. 66:1; **Jer. 23:23, 24**; Acts 17:27, 28; **Eph. 1:23**)

Wise:

To have all knowledge used correctly and well. (Ps. 92:5; 136 (all); **Prov. 2:6,7**; Isa. 55:8; Jer. 10:12; **Dan. 2:20–23**; **Rom. 11:33–34**; 16:27; Eph. 1:17; **Col. 2:1–3**; James 1:5)

All-knowing:

To be in possession of all there is to understand past, present, future, including those things that are impossible. God never learns anything new nor has He been taught by anyone. (Job 38:3;40:3; **Ps. 33:13–15**; 139:11–12; 147:5 Prov. 15:3; Isa. 40:12–31; **46:10**; Rom. 11:33–34; Heb. 4:13; 1 John 3:20)

Holy:

Complete freedom from any sin, evil, or wrong. Pure with absolute moral perfection. Holiness is a standard set by God's own nature and not something externally imposed on Him. The quality of holiness of God is unique to Him. (Note: the Spirit of God is called the Holy Spirit.) (**Lev. 20:26; 1 Sam. 2:2; Ps. 18:30; 99:9; Isa. 6:1–5; Ezek. 39:25; 1 Thess. 4:8; 1 Peter 1:15–16; Rev. 15:4**)

King:

Absolute Ruler of everything and everyone in all the universe. (Ex. 15:18; **Ps. 47:2; 93:2; 1 Tim. 1:17; 6:15–16; Heb. 1:8;** Rev. 15:3)

Eternal:

Having no beginning and no end. (**Deut. 33:27;** Ps. 9:7; **90:1–2; 93:2; 102:12, 24–27;** Isa. 57:15; **Hab. 1:12; Rom. 1:20;** 1 Tim. 1:17; **Heb. 9:14**)

Infinite:

Not limited by anything including time, space, or quantity. In speaking about an essential attribute of God, it refers to His unlimited existence, perfection, capacity, and energy. (**1 Kings 8:27; 2 Chron. 6:18; Job 11:7–9;** Ps. 147:5; Isa. 40:25; 46:5,9–10; **Jer. 23:24;** Heb. 6:13; Rev. 1:17,18)

LEVEL 2: SACRIFICIAL SAVIOR

Good:

To be upright, righteous, beneficial. (**2 Chron. 5:13;** Ezra 3:11; **Ps. 25:8; 27:13; 33:5; 52:1; 100:5; 106:1; 107:1;** Matt. 5:43–45; **Rom. 2:4**)

Loving:

Love that is unchanging, not based on who we are but who He is and His nature of being love itself. (**2 Chron. 5:13;** Ps.

86:5,15; 100:5; 106:1; 107:8; 145:17; Jer. 31:3; Lam.
3:22–23; John 3:16; Rom. 5:8; 8:35, 38–39; Titus 3:4; 1 John
3:1-3; 4:8)

¶ 3:5

Caring:

Concern and interest in you personally and in every detail
of your life. (Isa. 54:10; 64:5; Ezek. 34:12; Zeph. 3:17; Matt.
6:25–34; 10:29–31; Heb. 4:16)

Merciful:

Withholding punishment deserved and giving kindness in
excess. (Note: Observe quantity and quality of God's mercy.)
(Ex. 34:6; Num. 14:18; Ps. 13:5; 25:6,10; 103:17; Luke
1:78,79; Eph. 2:4; 1 Pet. 1:3)

Sacrificial:

The free choice by the Godhead wherein, because of their
great love for and value placed on mankind, God the Father and
God the Holy Spirit allowed God the Son to become a human
in order to live a perfect life on earth. This led to fulfilling their
plans for Him to become a substitute for human beings through
His death on the cross, in order to pay for the sin of everyone.
This included the additional sacrifice of the Son, not availing
Himself of His rights as Deity while here on earth and the
corresponding sacrifice of the Trinity not having interaction
with each other in the same way as prior to the incarnation of
Jesus. (Isa. 53:4–7; Luke 9:20–22; John 1:1, 2, 14; 3:16; Rom.
3:25; Eph. 2:4–10; Phil. 2:6–9; 1 Peter 1:18–21; 3:18)

Forgiving:

To pardon completely and give up punishment for all sin
and never bring up the offenses again. In this case, the forgiveness is given only when the God-given substitute and payment
for sin is accepted by the sinner. (Ex. 34:6–7; Num. 14:18; Ps.
32:1–5; 51 (all); 86:5, 15; 103:3–4; Isa. 1:18; 43:25; Eph.
1:7–8; 1 John 1:9)

Accepting:

Giving approval without conditions. (Ps. 103:8–14; Matt. 11:28; Rom. 5:8; Eph. 1:6, KJV; 2:8–9; Titus 3:5)

Intermediator:

Being a bridge between Holy God and sinful man to provide a way for sinful man to be in God's presence. (Eph. 2:14–18; 3:12; 1 Tim. 2:5; Heb. 8:6; 9:15; 12:24)

Gentle:

Courteous, kind, patient, even-tempered, not abrasive, harsh, or cruel. (Ps. 34:18; Matt. 11:28, 29; 21:5; John 8:1–11; 2 Cor. 10:1; Gal. 5:22)

LEVEL 3: LOVING FATHER

Protector:

Guards, shields, and defends from everything that can try to harm. (Ps. 3: (all); 18: (all); 32:6–7; 33:18; 34:1–10,15, 19; 37:28; 41:2; 46:1–7; 55:18; 59:16–17; 91 and 121: (all); Isa. 43:2; 54:10; 2 Thess. 3:3; 2 Tim. 1:12; 4:17,18)

Provider:

To provide or supply our every need. (Ps. 23: (all); 34:10; Mark 11:22–24; John 15:7; Rom. 8:32; 2 Cor. 9:8; Phil. 1:6; 4:19; Heb. 4:16; Jas. 1:5,17)

Patient:

Extending grace far beyond the usual time by waiting or enduring without complaint or reprisal. (Ex. 34:6–7; Num. 14:18; Ps. 86:15; Rom. 2:4; Eph. 5:9; 1 Tim. 1:16; 1 Pet. 3:20; 2 Pet. 3:9)

Teacher / Discipler:

Instructing us in how to live. Jesus often is the Model for this. (Ps. 25:4–5, 9; 27:11; 32:8; 48:14; Isa. 48:17; 50:4; John 3:2; Acts 1:1; Phil. 1:6)

Helper:

Coming along side to assist in whatever is needed. (Ps. 27:9; 30:10; **33:20**; 37:39, 40;**40:**13, 17; 46:1–3; 121: (all); **Isa. 41:10**, 13; 54:1–4; **Heb. 4:16**; 13:5,6)

Caring:

Deep interest in all that concerns you. (**Ps. 71:20**, 21; 103:8–14, 17; Matt. 6:25–34; Eph. 2:4–6; 1 Pet. 5:7)

Accessible:

Giving the right to enter or approach at any time. He is close to us. (Ps. 22:11, 19; 34:18; 145:18–20; Jer. 23:23, 24; Acts 17:27,28; Rom. 5:1,2; Eph. 2:14–18; 3:12; Phil. 4:5; Heb. 4:16)

Kind:

Sympathetic, gentle, warm-hearted response. (Ps. 34:18; **Isa. 63:7**; Luke 6:35; **Rom. 2:4**; Titus 3:4)

Unchanging:

Reliable, consistent, steady, always the same. (**Ps. 33:11**; **Isa. 14:24**; 40:8; Mal. 3:6; Heb. 13:8; Jas. 1:17)

LEVEL 4: FAITHFUL COMPANION

Fair and just:

To do what is right without partiality. (**Deut. 10:17** Isa. 61:8; Acts 10:34–35; Rom. 2:6,11; Eph. 6:8; 3:25; Heb. 6:10; 1 Pet. 1:17; **Rev. 15:3**)

Compassionate:

To have pity, empathize with, be touched by, have mercy on. (**Ezra 9:13**; Ps. 34:18; 78:38; 86:15; 103:13; 111:4; Prov. 25:2; Isa. 54:10; Lam. 3:22–23; Matt. 9:36; 15:32; 20:34; Luke 13:34; Heb. 4:15)

Wonderful:

Marvelous, exceedingly good, excellent, fine, admirable. (Ex. 15:11; Ps. 33; 35:10;71:19; 139:6; Isa. 9:6; 25:1; Matt. 21:15; Acts 2:11; Rev. 15:3)

Encourager:

To give support, help, and confidence (Deut. 31:6–8; Ps. 17:8; 34:18; Isa. 41:13; 2 Thess. 2:16–17)

Peace Giver:

God, who is peace—the absence of disorder with calm, quiet tranquillity—gives us His peace. (Ps. 29:11; 119:165; Isa. 9:6; 26:3, 12; Micah 5:5; John 14:27; 16:33; Rom. 1:7; 15:33; Gal. 5:22; Eph. 2:14; Phil. 4:6–9; Col. 3:15; 2 Thess. 3:16)

Counselor:

Gives perfect guidance and advice from a position of having all knowledge and wanting the best for us. (Ps. 16:7; 32:8–9; 48:4; 73:24; 119:9, 24; Prov. 3:5; Isa. 9:6; 30:21; 58:11; John 16:13)

Faithful:

Constant, loyal, keeping promises and commitments. (Ps. 23; 31:19; 89:1–2,5,8,14,24,28,33; 119:90; Isa. 25:1; 46:11; Lam. 3:22–23; Rom. 8:28; 1 Cor. 10:13; 1 Thess. 5:24; 2 Thess. 3:3; 2 Tim. 2:13; James 1:17; 1 John 1:9)

Empowerer:

Gives you the power to live the Christian life successfully. (Ps. 18:29; Isa. 40:29; 1 Cor. 10:13; Eph. 1:19; 3:20; 6:10–17; Phil. 1:6; 2:12–13; 4:13; 2 Thess. 1:11; 2:16–17; 3:3)

Giving:

To bestow on us things which we need that we have not earned. (Ps. 84:11; 119:30; Prov. 3:34; Isa. 40:29; Luke 11:9–10; John 3:16; Acts 11:17; Eph. 2:7; 3:20; Phil. 4:19; 1 Pet. 1:4; 1 John 5:11)

Trustworthy:

Worthy of our confidence because He is honest, dependable, faithful with integrity. (Ps. 4:5; 9:10; 25:9,10; 27:13; 37:3–5; 52:8; 56:3–11; 111:7; 138:8; Jer. 22:9–11; 29:11; Heb. 2:13)

LEVEL 5: GOOD FRIEND

Note: There is some overlapping from here on of previous information because you will be discovering much deeper truths of these characteristics of God.

Great wisdom:

(See Wise under level 1.) (Isa. 55:8; Jer. 33:3; Col. 1:9)

Perfection:

Without flaw, pure, complete and with an extreme degree of excellence. (Deut. 32:4; 2 Sam. 22:31; Ps. 18:30; 19:7; Matt. 5:48)

Tough Love-Giver:

Loving us perfectly, but in so doing, holding us to a high standard which He helps us reach. (Ps. 118:18; Is. 38:17; Matt. 6:24; 7:12; Luke 12:47–48; John 15:1, 2; Rom. 2:1–6; Eph. 3:12; Heb. 12:5; 1 Pet. 1:6–7; 5:6)

Purity:

Without anything wrong. (Deut. 32:4; Job 4:17; 34:10; Ps. 12:6; 18:26; 33; 43:5; Prov. 30:5; Hab. 1:13)

Great faithfulness:

(See Faithfulness under level 4.) (1 Chron. 16:34; Ps. 116:6, 12; 117:2; Prov. 2:8; Isa. 26:3,4; 65:24; Jer. 29:11; Phil. 1:6)

Gracious:

Being merciful, kind, loving, and compassionate . (Ex. 34:6; 2 Chron. 30:9; Neh. 2:8; 9:17; Ps. 86:15; 116:5; Isa. 30:18; 2 Thess. 2:16–17)

Unselfish:

Not stingy, considering the good of others as a high priority, often in a sacrificial way. (John 3:16; Heb. 12:2–3)

Unchanging:

To stay in an original position or to maintain the same direction. (1 Sam. 15:29; Mal. 3:6; James 1:17)

Dependable:

Reliable, trustworthy, and keeps word. (Ps. 34:10; 105:8,42; Phil. 1:6; 2 Thess. 3:3)

Comforter:

Encouragement and support-giver, especially in a stressful or troubled time. (Ps. 34:18; Isa. 51:12; 61:2; John 14:16,26; Acts 9:31; 2 Cor. 1:3)

LEVEL 6: INTIMATE FRIEND

Tender hearted:

Easily moved to love, compassion, pity, or sorrow. (Ps. 25:6; 34:18; 40:11; 116:15; 145:9; Isa. 40:11; Zeph. 3:17; Matt. 23:37)

Very gentle:

See definition and level 2 material on Gentle (Ps. 103:13; Isa. 40:11; 2 Cor. 10:1)

Great heart of love:

See definition and verses under level 2. (Ps. 17:7; 32:10; 36:5–7; 63:3; 103:11; 108:4;130:7; Isa. 30:18; 54:10; 63:7; 64:4; Jer. 31:3; Zeph. 3:17; Eph. 1:7–8; 2: 4; 3:16–19; 1 John 3:1)

Complete ability to meet every need and care:

(2 Sam. 22:29; Ps. 20 and 23 (all); 55:22; 68:19; 107:9; 138:8; Isa. 26:3; Eph. 3:20; 2 Thess. 2:16–17; 1 Pet. 5:7)

Absolute Sovereign and in total control:

(1 Chron. 29:11, 12; Job 23:13; Ps. 2 and 8; 18:28, 29; 27:13; 33:11; 71:19; Prov. 19:21)

Awesome:

Inspiring overwhelmingly great respect, reverence, and healthy fear for the greatness, majesty, and works of God. (Ex. 15:11; Deut. 7:21; 10:17, 21; Job 25:2; Ps. 22:23; 47:2; 68:35; Dan. 9:4; Eph. 3:20; 1 Tim. 6:15)

Absolutely trustworthy:

(Ps. 17:2; 18:25–26; 71:5,6,19–21; 138:8; 145:13–20; 2 Thess. 1:6)

Totally good:

See definition and verses under level 2. Added to this is the fact that God is only good, in contrast to the temptations we receive to question His goodness, His care for us, or His motives towards us. (Ps. 25:8; 33:4; 34:8; 116:7, 12; 118:1; Jer. 29:11)

Wants the very best for me:

(Ps. 3:3; 32:8; 35:27; 103:1–5; Isa. 58:11; Jer. 29:11; Eph. 1:3; James 1:17; 2 Pet. 1:3, 4)

Is completely committed to me:

(Deut. 31:8; Ps. 17:8; 37:4, 23–24,28,37; 40:5; 94:14; 112:4; 138:8; 147:11; Isa. 30:18, 21; 46:3–4; Jer. 29:11; Rom. 8:31–32; 2 Thess. 2:16; 2 Tim. 3:16–17; 1 Pet. 1:3–5)

Note: Although there are many other qualities of God, such as being invisible, we do not focus on them as much when drawing closer to Him and are therefore not listed here. However, no attribute or quality of God is insignificant. Each should be studied as you become aware of them.

◆

Removing Hindrances
to Fellowship with God

At Levels 1 and 2

Write down your reservations and questions. Ask God to reveal the truth to you, then go to the end of the chapter and look up the verses listed. See if any of the Scriptures answer your questions. It would also be helpful for you to look at some of the other attributes / character qualities listed in resource 1.

If you still have reservations, turn to resource 3 and look for titles of additional books on the subject that is giving you trouble. The suggestions for levels 3 through 6 may also hold a solution, so investigate that material.

Finally, if you still can not find the answer to your questions or reservations, write us. Enclose a stamped, self-addressed #10 envelope, and use the address in the "How to Use This Book" section. We will try to answer you in a timely manner.

—

LEVELS 3 THROUGH 6

In order for this process to be effective, you need to be absolutely honest with yourself. The Holy Spirit will show you things—some you may not want to hear or feel are too insignificant. But nothing is too small to become a hindrance, so it is best to do these steps with paper and pencil and covenant before the Lord that you will write down whatever He shows you, no matter what. Only then will you truly be able to wrestle with your hindrances and have God's victory.

Part 1

1. Try to identify the hindrance in your fellowship with God. Read chapter 9. Especially note and follow Action step DT-2. See also the list of enemy attacks at the end of the chapter.

2. If you still feel there is a hindrance, you may also want to review the "What Happens When We Listen to Satan's Lies" starting in chapter 9 and then do Action step DT-3.

Part 2 if needed

1. Use resource 5 to expose and deal with any lies from the enemy. You may want to take the things you have already identified and put them on the chart.

2. Read through chapter 9: "What to Do in Dry Times."

Part 3 if needed

If you still sense problems, ask yourself the following questions:

1. What seems to be the thing that is keeping me from God?

2. Why am I "trapped" by it? Is there a lie I am believing that needs to be exposed? What attribute of God would solve this problem? (see resource 1) Is there a reason I do not believe God can solve this? Have I applied Romans 8:28 and 1 Thessalonians 5:16? Am I believing Philippians 4:13, 19? What excuses (lies) am I using not to trust God fully in this

area? (Note: Some lies of Satan are "This situation is different" or "You are not like others, so this doesn't apply to you"
or "You have done something that disqualifies you to apply
this promise.") (See action step DT-3.)

3. Am I violating a biblical principle? (See chap. 9)

4. Is there any unforgiveness, no matter how much the person
   is undeserving from a human perspective?

5. Do I have a critical spirit or do I gossip at all?

6. Do I have pride? Arrogance? Anger? A sharp tongue?

7. Am I letting the enemy cause me to fear doing what I know
   God wants?

Prayer of Commitment

Lord,
You know how hard it is for me to stop/give up
_____. Yet I know this is necessary if I am to
continue drawing closer to You. Help me, Holy Spirit, to
let You do what is necessary in me in order to remove this
hindrance. Once that happens, give me Your strength and
power and the courage to resist again the temptation
to_____.

Or the following might be appropriate:

Father,
I do not want to be deceived in any area of my life. I want
only to believe the truth, no matter what it may be. Please
help me to recognize the lies of the enemy, his temptations
to doubt You, others and myself along with any fears he may
bring. Holy Spirit, then tell me what the truth is. Show me
from the Word Your perspective on whatever is in question.

♦

Bibliography with Selected Annotations

The Nature of God (including the Trinity) and Bible Analysis and Helps

Bailey, Waylon, and Tom Hudson. *Step by Step Through the Old Testament*. Nashville: Lifeway, 1991. Thirteen-unit self-instructional workbook survey of the Old Testament.

Blackaby, Henry, and Claude V. King. *Experiencing God Bible*. Nashville: Broadman & Holman, 1994. Experience-related, God-centered Bible study, NKJV version.

Boice, James Montgomery. *The Sovereign God*. Madison, Wis.: Inter-Varsity Press, 1978.

Disciples Study Bible. Nashville: Broadman & Holman, 1988. Focuses on intensive study of twenty-seven great doctrines; NIV version.

Erickson, Millard J. *Christian Theology*. Grand Rapids, Mich.: Baker Book House, 1983–85. Evangelical systematic theology.

Grenz, Stanley. *Theology for the Community of God*. Nashville: Broadman & Holman, 1994. A very readable evangelical theology.

Lea, Thomas D., and Tom Hudson. *Step by Step Through the New Testament.* Nashville: Lifeway, 1992. Thirteen-unit self-instructional workbook survey of the New Testament.

Lea, Thomas D. *How to Study Your Bible.* Nashville: Convention Press, 1986. Eleven weeks of daily instruction dealing with interpretation and helps.

Little, Paul E. *Know What You Believe.* Wheaton Ill.: Victor Press, 1988. Classic on basic Christianity including the reliability of Scriptures, nature of God, the Trinity, salvation, etc.

Lockyer, Herbert, D.D. *All the Divine Names and Titles in the Bible.* Grand Rapids, Mich.: Zondervan Publishing House, 1975.

Nave, Orville J. *Nave's Topical Bible.* McLean, Va.: Mac Donald Publishing Co, n.d. A classic topical book with appropriate important KJV verses written under each heading.

New Bible Commentary, 21st-century edition. Madison, Wis.: InterVarsity Press, 1994. Considered one of the best one-volume Bible commentaries.

The New Strong's Exhaustive Concordance. Nashville, Tenn.: Nelson, 1991. Every word in the King James Version of the Bible is listed within its context along with the Greek or Hebrew word and meanings. (Other publishers have NIV and NASB version concordances.)

Packer, J. I. *Knowing God.* Madison, Wis.: InterVarsity Press, 1973. Important classic.

Willis, Avery Jr. *Bible Guide to Discipleship and Doctrine.* Nashville: Broadman & Holman, 1991. Helps adults learn how to use the Bible to gain insights into doctrines and disciplines.

General Teachings on Prayer and Quiet Time Guidelines

Beltz, Bob. *Transforming Your Prayer:* A 7-week strategy to a more meaningful relationship with God. Brentwood: Tenn.: Wolgemuth & Hyatt, 1991.

Bounds, E.M. *The Necessity of Prayer.* Grand Rapids, Mich.: Baker Book House, 1976. A classic on various factors in prayer as well as the mystery and majesty of prayer.

Duewel, Wesley. *Mighty Prevailing Prayer.* Grand Rapids, Mich.: Zondervan, 1990.

Christenson, Evelyn, and Viola Blake. *What Happens When Women Pray.* Wheaton, Ill.: Victor Books, 1976. A classic on prayer results from the average lay person.

Gentile, Earnest B. *Awaken the Dawn.* San Jose, Calif.: Bible Temple Publishing, 1990. (1-800-777-6057) Good material for developing your own personal quiet time.

Hunt, T. W., and Claude V. King. *In God's Presence.* Nashville: Lifeway, 1995. Six weeks of daily study and practice.

Hunt, T. W. *Disciple's Prayer Life: Walking in Fellowship with God.* Nashville: Lifeway, 1988. Strengthens and deepens prayer life, based on prayers in the Bible.

Hybles, Bill. *Too Busy Not to Pray.* Downers Grove, Ill.: Inter-Varsity Press, 1986.

Lea, Larry. *Could You Not Tarry One Hour?* Altamonte Springs, Fla.: Creation House, 1987. Uses the Lord's Prayer as a format for spending an hour in prayer.

Murray, Andrew. *With Christ in the School of Prayer.* Old Tappan, N.J.: Revell, 1953. A classic. Must reading.

Prayer for Those Who Influence Your Family. Prayerworks, 24600 Arrowhead Springs Road, San Bernardino, Calif. 92414.

Stanley, Charles F. *Handle with Prayer.* Wheaton, Ill.: Victor Books, 1986. Prayer principles: avoiding enemy attacks, praying while waiting, praying God's will, intercession, etc.

Drawing Closer to God

Blackaby, Henry, and Claude V. King. *Experiencing God.* Nashville: Lifeway, 1990. Knowing and doing the will of God.

———. *Fresh Encounter: God's Pattern for Revival and Spiritual Awakening.* Nashville: Lifeway, 1993. Six-week study of revival from a biblical and historical perspective.

Dawson, Joy. *Intimate Friendship with God.* Old Tappan, N.J.: Revell, 1986.

Eastman, Dick. *A Celebration of Praise.* Grand Rapids, Mich.: Baker Book House, 1984. Surveys different facets of God's person in order to praise the true depth of God's nature.

Hayford, Jack W. *Prayer Is Invading the Impossible.* Plainfield, N.J.: Logos International, 1977. A "how to" book on strengthening inner faith needed for prayer.

————. *Worship His Majesty.* Dallas, Tex.: Word Publishers, 1987. A classic on worship, emphasizing the focus of worship being on God and the power worship has to change people.

Hunt , T.W., and Claude V. King. *The Mind of Christ.* Nashville: Lifeway, 1994. How to have the mind of Christ, based on Philippians 2:5–11.

Kern, Deborah. *Near to the Heart of God.* Eugene, Oreg.: Harvest House Publishers, 1993. Helpful suggestions for intimacy with God for those already seeking such a relationship.

Klug, Ronald. *How to Keep a Spiritual Journal.* Nashville: Thomas Nelson, 1982.

Ogilvie, Lloyd John. *Conversation with God: Experience Intimacy with God through Personal Prayer.* Eugene, Oreg.: Harvest House Publishers, 1993.

Stanley, Charles. *How to Listen to God.* Nashville: Oliver Nelson Books, 1985. Includes how to distinguish God's voice from other sources.

Fasting and Spiritual Warfare

Alves, Elizabeth. *The Mighty Warrior.* Bulverde, Tex.: Canopy Press, 1992. Excellent. Includes purpose of prayer, types, hearing from God, spiritual warfare, and weapons of warfare.

Beall, James Lee. *The Adventure of Fasting.* Old Tappan N.J.: Fleming H. Revell Co., 1974. Practical guidebook on fasting, answering many questions.

Jacobs, Cindy. *Possessing the Gates of the Enemy.* Tarrytown, N.Y.: Chosen Books, 1991. In-depth intercession strategies, as well as common pitfalls to avoid in prayer.

Wagner, C. Peter. *Prayer Shield.* Ventura, Calif.: Regal Books, 1992. How to intercede for pastors, Christian leaders, and others on the spiritual front lines.

Wallis, Arthur. *God's Chosen Fast.* Fort Washington, Pa.: Christian Literature Crusade, 1968. Deals with all the main fasting passages in Scripture and the practical issues involved.

White, Thomas B. *The Believer's Guide to Spiritual Warfare.* Ann Arbor, Mich.: Servant Publications, 1990. Invaluable handbook on resisting enemy attacks.

Prayer for Evangelization, Missions, and the World

Duewel, Wesley L. *Touch the World through Prayer.* Grand Rapids, Mich.: Zondervan, 1986. Powerful book on effectiveness of prayer for evangelism and how to use it in your life.

Eastman, Dick. *Love on Its Knees.* Old Tappan, N.J.: Chosen Books, 1989. Principles of intercession for praying for peoples of the world and your loved ones.

Johnstone, Patrick. *Operation World.* 5th ed. Pasadena, Calif.: William Carey Library, 1993. Excellent handbook for all countries of the world giving religious, political, and economic information and prayer requests.

Video

Orr, Dr. J. Edwin. "The Role of Prayer in Spiritual Awakening." San Bernardino, Calif.: Inspirational Media. A powerful twenty-six minute video by one of the foremost authorities on the subject of prayer and revival. Shows how God has used average praying people to help start revival both in the United States and abroad. Stirring examples are given of different revivals and their impact on morality and society. Can be ordered for $25, which includes postage and handling. Make checks payable to Dian Ginter. Send to 2683, Holly Vista Blvd., Highland, CA 922346 or call 909-862-3467.

♦

Charting Your Growth

*C*opy the following items into a chart for your notebook. Be sure to leave enough space between each item. Then once a quarter (or more if you wish) do a check-up on your spiritual growth. The items listed are the fruit of the Spirit as listed in Galatians 5: 22–23 plus a few other growth indicators. Personalize the chart by adding your own areas of concern and those things the Lord shows you that need work. Honesty will be the only way to make this a useful tool.

As you see progress, thank the Lord for it. When you find you are stuck and not growing in an area, ask His help. Do not let this chart become a burden for you. Let it be an encouragement and a way of keeping yourself accountable before the Lord.

Rank your growth in each period on a scale of 0 to 10, with 10 being perfect. Under "Observations" note anything about this area the Lord has shown you, perhaps the reasons you struggle with it. You may also fill out a separate "Area to Work On" page (resource 9) for each area you identify as in need of improvement. If you feel comfortable in doing so, set a goal for a specific date. This will help you keep on target in your growth. If you fail to reach that target, reevaluate why, and consider reading some Christian books on the subject. Talk to others who have the quality you are needing improvement in and see how they handle it; especially important is their thought life when tempted to fail in this area. What do they do to resist the temptation to _____? At the end of the chart, you may want to set some goals for this year, and note new ones for next year.

♦

My Growth Chart For 19___

Area	January 1	April 1	July 1	October 1	Verses	Goals / Observations
Love						
Joy						
Peace						
Patience						
Kindness						
Gentleness						
Faithfulness						
Meekness						
Bible Study						
Prayer Life						
Sharing Faith						
Trust in God						
Closeness to God						

The Names of God

Yahweh-Roi–"The Lord, my Shepherd"
Yahweh-Jireh–"The Lord shall provide"
Yahweh-Shalom–"The Lord our peace"
Yahweh-Rophe–"The Lord our healer"
Yahweh-Tsidkenu–"The Lord our righteousness"
Yahweh-Nissi–"The Lord my banner"
Yahweh-Shammah–"The Lord is there"
Yahweh-Mekaddishkhem–"The Lord that sanctifies you"
El Shaddai–"The God who supplies my needs"
El Elyon–"Possessor of heaven and earth"
El Olam–"The everlasting God"
El Gibbor–"The mighty God"
Yahweh-Melek–"The God who is King"
Yahweh-Sabaoth–"The Lord of hosts"
Adonai–"The Lord/Master"
Elohim–"God"
Yahweh–"Lord"
Pater–"Father"

Steps to Knowing
God's Will

Step 1. Obey what God has already revealed in the Bible. This is an absolute prerequisite because it demonstrates our submission and openness.

Step 2. Commit to the importance of God's Word in your life for guidance. The Bible is unquestionably the most important avenue for evaluating our beliefs and actions. Thus, we must become Bereans (Acts 17:11) who have attentive and open hearts to learn.

Step 3. Pray. If you ever desire to know God's perfect will you must have an active prayer life. How can you expect God to guide you if you are not listening?

Step 4. Trust the Holy Spirit's leading. Jesus tells us that the Holy Spirit is given to every believer (John 14:16–17; Rom. 8:14). But we are later commanded to be filled with the Holy

Spirit (Eph. 5:18). God wants to fill us with the Holy Spirit as we learn day-by-day to allow Him to control more areas of our lives. (See information starting in chapter 4.)

Step 5. Counsel with other trusted believers. Our primary counsel must be from God's Word. However, at times God uses the counsel of other people to help us to know His will.

Step 6. Evaluate recent circumstances. God provides providential circumstances to guide us and motivate us. There are opportunities in our lives which we must not take lightly in seeking God's will. However, if circumstances contradict the Bible's guidance, choose the Bible every time.

Step 7. Decide and wait for God's peace. God's peace will be the stamp of approval.

♦

Various Prayers

CONTROL OF TONGUE

Lord Jesus,
You know how easy it is for me to say the first thing that comes into my mind in a difficult situation. I often have an out-of-control tongue. I know that this hurts You as well as others and that You want me to say only edifying things. I am asking You to take control of my thoughts and my tongue. Help me not to say hurtful things or use words that may be misunderstood even when I am not aware there may be a problem. Holy Spirit, whenever I am tempted to use my tongue wrongly, bring this situation to my attention, and give me the power to stop before I say anything negative. Then give me Your response. Help me keep my emotions under control and recognize when the enemy wants me to believe a wrong idea. Keep me believing only the truth about others and myself as well as my circumstances.

or

Lord,
I really need Your self-control with my tongue when I'm
talking to my family. Help me be a calm person when I talk
to my kids. Help me be consistent with them and to do it
in a loving way. Give me a calm and quiet spirit.

TEMPTATION TO DO OR THINK WRONGLY

Lord,
Right now I feel like_____ which I know I should not
do. I feel weak. Help me not to do this by giving me Your
strength to resist. You have said in Philippians 4:13 that I
can do all things through Jesus who strengthens me. Help
me, Jesus. Give me the courage and ability to do what You
are showing me to do.

KEEPING EYES ON JESUS IN TIMES OF TROUBLE

Lord,
Show me how to live on top of my circumstances and not
under them. Help me keep my eyes on You, Lord Jesus,
instead of on my problems. Let me see You, Father, as the
One who can and will meet every need of my life. Let me
be sufficient in You and not in my own abilities and
strengths. Help me have the right balance between living
in Your control and exercising diligence in responding to
each facet of my life. Whenever pressures come that have
been unbearable or debilitating before, show me Your
perspective—anything I've been doing wrong, thinking
improperly. Then show me how to correct my faulty actions
and thoughts so that I can continue to walk in Your Spirit's
control and have victory. Thank You for wanting these
things in my life even more than I do. Remind me of that
when my faith gets weak.

COMMITMENT AND SUBMISSION TO GOD

Father,

I want to do what You show me is the right thing to do. As we both know, that is not always what happens. But I am asking You to change me; to show me how to submit to You, to reveal to me anything which is causing me to hold back from completely yielding to Your will. Then help me do whatever is necessary to do what You want. I love You and trust You. (See next prayer for more ideas in this area.)

SUBMISSION TO GOD BY SUBMITTING TO OTHERS

Father,

I want to be submissive to those You have put over me, to think of others as better than myself. But frankly speaking, this scares me. It makes me feel so vulnerable and out of control. I know You are in charge and can make people respond as You wish. But (name of person) seems so _____, so capable of hurting me or taking advantage of me , of not being worthy of my trust. My past experience with him/her has been so bad that it bothers me to think of submitting to him/her. But at the same time, I know this is what You are asking me to do. I want to be obedient to You, but I am finding it very difficult to take this step. Yet I am willing to do so. [or you may need to pray: *Please make me willing to do so.*] *Give me the courage to take charge of our relationship and let me be safe in submitting. Help me not to fear and not to want my own way to the degree that I will not submit out of fear and/or the need to be in control of my own life. I know I am not supposed to be in such control. But, oh, Lord, it is so hard to turn loose of what I have been so protective of all these years—me! Give me courage and the right attitude in this situation. Show me where I am not trusting You fully and why. Then show me how to overcome this. Give me Scrip-*

ture to break the lie(s) I've been believing. Help me trust You enough to take this step. How I need your help if I am going to be able to do this. But in my heart of hearts I want to. It is only my insecurity and lack of complete trust in You that keeps me from taking it. Show me what I need in order to trust You in this area enough to take this step.

AFTER SINNING OR FALLING

Lord,
I've blown it again. I did not act in submission/love/patience, etc. when I _____. Please forgive me and show me what I've done wrong that allowed me to fail. (self-centered? wanted own way? did not submit? pride? control? anger?) *Where did my thinking go wrong? What did I do to allow this to happen? How should I have responded? Please help me know the truth and show me how to avoid doing this again. What Scripture can I apply?*

WHEN SOMEONE DOES SOMETHING TO OFFEND YOU

Lord,
I choose not to take offense at what _____ said/did. I choose to forgive him/her for his/her words/actions. Help me forget this and focus on You. Thank You that You are kind and loving and gentle and accept me just as I am. How I love and trust You!

ASKING FOR ZEAL TO DO GOD'S WILL

Lord,
I desire to have a zeal for Your will in the same way Jesus had a zeal for Your House. Consume me with such desire to do what You want me to do, so that I will sacrifice anything for it. May the zeal of Your will consume me!

◆

How Effectively to Put on the Armor of God

We are in a daily battle, whether we know it or not. That is why in Ephesians 6 we are told to "put on the full armor of God" (v. 11). Just as a soldier gets dressed each day, as Christians we too need to put on spiritual clothing each morning. But for many putting on the armor of God has become a routine akin to a magical incantation and similar to how some pray the Lord's Prayer. Instead it should be a well-thought-out, purposeful process which helps prepare us for whatever may come in our day. The difference between the two lies in what we are thinking as we "put on the armor."

Become familiar with this armor before you put it on. First of all, you may have noticed that all elements of the armor and what they represent actually describe the nature of Jesus. For example, He is our salvation, righteousness, and peace. He is truth and the Word of God. Most of the armor is a protection, a covering of the vital parts of our body so that when the enemy attacks, he cannot touch us. We may not stop the attack, but we can stop any wounding. The Sword is our only truly offensive piece. But, oh, how powerful it is! When you skillfully combine the Word of God (the Sword) with faith (the Shield), you have an unbeatable protection against whatever attacks the enemy may hurl at you during your day's "battle."

For ease of memory, we put on the armor from top to bottom. The following is a suggested prayer for putting on your armor each morning before you go out into your particular battles. You will find that several go somewhat beyond the standard "putting on of the armor" since they are scriptural extensions of the basics of each piece of armor. Feel free to adapt this to fit your particular way of expressing yourself and the needs of your day's agenda.

HELMET OF SALVATION

Understanding Its Purpose:

There are three tenses of "salvation": past, present and future. We are saved from the penalty of sin already (past). In the present we need salvation from the power of sin which is what the helmet is for. In the future we will be saved from the presence of sin.

The helmet covers our mind. All sin of any kind originates in the mind: rebellion, lying, lust, murder, rejection of God, wrong thoughts, etc. Our words are spoken only after they have gone through our mind. Therefore, if we can keep all of our thoughts under the control of Jesus, as we are told to do in 2 Corinthians 10:3–5, then sin will have no power over us. In other words, it will not have a chance to get a foothold, because we will have successfully resisted the temptation as we have brought that negative thought under the control of Jesus.

This means you need to first recognize the enemy's temptation, expose the lie he is telling you, and reject thinking about it any more. Often the Lord will bring Scripture to your mind (the Sword) to help in this process. Usually, lies of the enemy can be recognized by the fact that they cause you to think negatively about yourself or others (he is the accuser of the brethren) or to feel helpless, in despair, hopeless, depressed, useless, like a victim, filled with self-pity, or even suicidal.

Another tactic he uses is to make you question the goodness of God and His power, ability, or desire to help you or your worthiness of being helped by Him. He uses thoughts like, *If God really loved men, He wouldn't have let _____ happen* or *God really doesn't care about me very much. How could He? Look at what I've done. I've always been bad/weak/a failure/etc.*

Sample Prayer:

Lord,

I put on the helmet of salvation for You to protect me today from the power of sin. Keep the enemy from successfully tempting me in any way. Help me, Holy Spirit, to keep every thought under the control of the Lord Jesus. Help me today to recognize the temptations and lies of the enemy every time he tries to trick me or get me to believe a half-truth or be suspicious of someone. Let me think only Your thoughts. Control my tongue so that I speak only Your words. Let my words be positive and build up everyone. Let me only speak the truth and do so in Your love. Conform my will to Yours so that I only do what You want me to this day.

BREASTPLATE OF RIGHTEOUSNESS

Lord,

I put on Your righteousness to protect me in all I do today. Let everything I do be done in a right way. Let me be clean in all I do, say, or think. Let me walk in Your righteousness and not my own. Holy Spirit, show me anytime I am trying to live in my own goodness, strength, and abilities rather than Yours.

BELT OF TRUTH

Lord Jesus,
You are Truth. I therefore put on truth to cover every act,
every expression, every word I say. Help me not to compro-
mise or shade the truth in any way. Let Your truths be
foundational to all I do this day.

SHOES OF THE GOSPEL OF PEACE

Father,
I need the peace of Jesus to saturate all my day, to be part
of everything I do and say. I need His peace in my mind no
matter what the situation. As I look at You and not the
situation, let Your peace rule my heart and mind. Thank
You that You will help me to walk in peace throughout my
day. I am available to share Your peace with anyone with
whom You want me to do so.

SHIELD OF FAITH & SWORD OF THE SPIRIT

Lord,
Help me to use my shield of faith in a strong, effective way
to stop the fiery darts of the enemy in whatever form they
may take. As you show me his temptations, help me to use
my faith to resist and quench his attempts to make me doubt
You or to view myself or others in a negative way. Cause
my faith to be strengthened as I use it and as I see You and
who You are in each and every situation I encounter. Bring
to my mind appropriate verses to help quench every fiery
dart of the wicked one. Let Your Word be a sharp instrument
in my mouth to come against all the lies and deceptions of
the enemy.

THE WHOLE ARMOR OF GOD

Father,

As I walk through this day, let me walk in confidence that I am prepared for this day's battle, for I have on my armor. More importantly, I know that You who indwell me are greater than he who is in the world and is my enemy. Help me to remember that he is a defeated foe and only roars as a lion does, but he has had his teeth pulled; that he has no ability to touch me apart from Your permission. Let me know I am a victorious soldier in this warfare today because of who I am in Jesus and who He is in me. Thank You for the great confidence to face all this day will hold. I place this day in Your hands and give You permission to change my plans for this day in whatever way You see fit. May You be glorified in all I say and do this day.

◆

How to Close the Holes
in Your Armor

1. PRAY. PRAY. PRAY.

2. Recognize that the hole (weakness) is there.

3. Discover what area of God's nature you are not trusting in. Inevitably there is a lack of faith in God's ability involved in this hole.

4. Try to see in what ways the enemy attacks you. When are you vulnerable to his attacks? What sets it off? How are you failing to trust God in this area?

5. Confess the weakness as sin and ask forgiveness from God and, where appropriate, from anyone you have offended.

6. Ask the Lord to give you appropriate Scripture to claim to strengthen that area and to resist the attack of the enemy.

7. Request the Lord's help in bringing every thought under His control. Use 2 Corinthians 10:5 as your foundation.

8. Seek the Lord's help to strengthen your faith to understand which of His characteristics and promises are applicable to this weakness. Be certain to claim the truth of Philippians 4:13: "I can do all things through Him who strengthens me" (NASB).

Resources 8 are reprinted by permission of Broadman and Holman from the 1994 book *Power House* by Dr. Glen Martin and Dian Ginter. In *Power House* these are listed as resource 3A and 3B.

◆

Today's
Quiet Time Summary

Date: _____

Area of Bible Study: _____

New Thing(s) I Learned About:
    God _____
    Myself _____
    Others _____

I Want to Memorize: _____

Unanswered Question(s) From today: (put date and answer
when found.) _____

_____

Something I Would Like to study in the Future: _____

_____

A Special Promise/Truth from God to My Heart: _____

_____

Something I Need to Work on in My Life: _____

_____

—

Areas to Work On

Date: _____

Date Change Noted: _____

Area of Need/Current Response: _____

_____

Desired Response: _____

Hindrance(s) and Its Source(s): _____

What I Need to Do to Correct This: _____

Scripture I am claiming: _____

Prayer I Have Prayed Concerning This: _____

_____

_____

_____

_____

—